My Search

My Search

Josef Ben-Eliezer

Plough Publishing House

Published by Plough Publishing House
Walden, New York
Robertsbridge, England
Elsmore, Australia
www.plough.com

© 2013 by Plough Publishing House
All rights reserved.

Cover design by Olaf Johannson, spoon design, *www.spoondesign.de*
Cover photographs: *Above,* Josef Ben-Eliezer as a young man. Courtesy of
family collection. Copyright © 2015 by Plough Publishing House. *Below,*
children included in the Teheran *Kindertransport.* Copyright © USHMM.

ISBN 10: 0-87486-932-3
ISBN 13: 978-0-87486-932-3

A catalog record for this book is available from the British Library.
Library of Congress Cataloging-in-Publication Data

Ben-Eliezer, Josef, 1929- author.
  My search / Josef Ben-Eliezer.
     pages cm
  ISBN 978-0-87486-932-3 (pbk.)
  1. Ben-Eliezer, Josef, 1929- 2. Holocaust survivors--Biography. 3. Holocaust,
Jewish (1939-1945) 4. Bruderhof Communities. 5. Forgiveness. 6. Israel--
History--1948-1967. 7. Zionism. I. Title.
  D804.I75B46 2013
  940.53'18092--dc23
  [B]
                          2013041772

IN THIS GREAT CONFUSION there are innocent
people with pure hearts who are at a loss, shaken by
what they see, who ask with pain and sorrow: "Where
will our help come from? Who will guide us and give us
an example through their life, by their behavior? Who
can we follow?" Young and old search for true light with
deep longing, wrestling with their doubts.

Natan Hofshi, Israeli pacifist (1889–1980)

Contents

Grandmother, Lena, Judith, Mother, Uncle Milech, Josef, Leo

Foreword

ON AN EXCEPTIONALLY TENSE DAY in 1997, I sat in my office at Bethlehem Bible College as violent clashes between Israeli soldiers and Palestinian demonstrators escalated outside. The sound of heavy gunfire and the putrid smell of tear gas seeped in through my window.

But that's not why my hands trembled as I read a letter I had just opened. I have received countless letters in my lifetime, but this is one of the few I will always remember. In it, a woman named Channah Ben-Eliezer introduced herself as Josef Ben-Eliezer's daughter and shared some of her father's story.

As a Jewish child in Germany, Josef Ben-Eliezer experienced the Nazis' rise to power. His family first sought refuge in Poland, but was driven out when the Germans arrived. Josef fled eastward and ended up exiled to Siberia. He escaped and eventually came to Palestine, where he joined the brigades fighting to establish a Jewish state.

Their goal was to provide a safe haven for the persecuted Jews of Europe. Full of energy and enthusiasm, Josef found himself fighting with the forces that conquered the Palestinian town of Lydda, my hometown. (In this book, Josef refers to it by its Hebrew name, Lod.)

In her letter, Channah briefly described her father's account of the atrocities committed against the people of Lydda. The events of Lydda remain one of the open wounds in the relationship between Israeli Jews and Palestinians, as the majority of the town's inhabitants were forced to leave during the 1948 war. While this has been denied by many Israelis, reading about Josef's experiences confirmed what my father and other family members had told me.

For Josef, these events triggered flashbacks of being driven from his own home as a child – and started him on a lifelong spiritual quest for peace and reconciliation. This relentless search led him back to Germany, where he found brotherhood among a people that had committed horrible acts against his own people during the Holocaust. And now, decades later, it had led him to look for a way to reconcile with the Palestinians of Lydda and seek their forgiveness.

Channah's letter included a request. She wanted to help her father connect with people who had been expelled from their homes in Lydda. At the time, she did not know my family's story, only that I led an organization working for reconciliation between Jews and Palestinians.

This was a gift I would never have imagined – a man seeking forgiveness for an event that left scars and still very much affects the people of this land. I responded immediately to Josef's request and arranged for him to meet my father, Yacoub, in Lydda. When Josef arrived, I watched as they walked through the old city together, sharing their memories of that day in 1948. Then Josef turned to my father and asked his forgiveness. Later my father told me, "I never believed that my story would be acknowledged by a Jew, let alone by someone seeking forgiveness."

Some of the most difficult and challenging aspects in reconciliation initiatives between Israelis and Palestinians are history and narrative – what happened in this land, who is at fault, who started what, and how we choose to remember these events. For the Jews, there is the suffering and pain of the Holocaust and the discrimination they faced in the countries where they lived. For the Palestinians, the years 1947 to 1949, known as the *Nakba,* stand out in our memory, as many were uprooted from their homes and still have no nation to call home. All these events have left major scars that need to be acknowledged, understood, taken seriously, and addressed.

The story of Josef and Yacoub offers hope for all of us. It shows that once history and narrative are mutually recognized, there is indeed a way forward. It will require courage, openness, deep learning from life experiences, and a desire to move forward for the sake of a new generation. But like these two men, who rose above their own suffering, we too can find freedom and healing through repentance and forgiveness. May their act pave the way for many in our society.

Salim J. Munayer, PhD
Director, Musalaha, Jerusalem

1.

Earliest Memories

I WAS BORN IN JULY 1929, in Frankfurt, Germany. My parents were Eastern European Jews who had come several years earlier from Poland. Unlike the Jews who had lived in Germany for generations, they knew little or nothing about its culture – for example, about Goethe and Schiller. Most German Jews were wealthier and better educated. They were also patriotic; they considered themselves part of the country's middle-class society. But we did not feel so much at home.

At the time of my birth, my brother Leo was already eleven and my sister Lena ten. So for a year and a half, I was the baby in the family. Even after my younger sister, Judith, was born, I received a lot of attention, because I was often sick. My parents had established a fairly comfortable living by then, so I was pretty spoiled as a child. We shared a house with several relatives from my mother's family, and I used to play with my cousins.

My parents had a kind of warehouse together with my uncle, Chaim Simcha. In Germany at that time, young Jewish women often used the income from their first job for an *Aussteuer* – a set of sheets, pillows and blankets, and maybe even a featherbed – for the day when they would marry. My father and uncle sold such sets of linens to be paid off in monthly installments. The business went well, and our extended family acquired several properties in Frankfurt. So we were fortunate that we had the means to escape Germany when the Nazis came to power.

My memories of Frankfurt are varied and scattered: an exciting visit to the zoo, dreadful throat examinations in kindergarten, and a fantastic candy shop around the corner from our house.

My first encounter with anti-Semitism was my mother's horror when I came home and used, in front of her, the expression *Dreckjude* – "dirty Jew." As a three-year-old, I must have picked it up from playmates without understanding what it meant. A short time later, we watched from the windows of our house as the Hitler's S.A. (*Sturm Abteilung,* or "Storm Troops") marched through the street singing, "When Jewish blood spurts from our knives . . ." More than my own fear, I remember the look of terror in my parents' eyes.

When Hitler came to power in January 1933, my parents were convinced that we needed to leave Germany. In April, Father went to Palestine to find a home for us there. We waited anxiously for news; eight months we waited. But in the end he could not secure permission from the British authorities for us to enter Palestine. He sent word that we should meet him in Poland, because he felt it was unsafe for him to return to Germany. After a joyful reunion at the train station in Rzeshov, we made our way to my mother's hometown of Rozwadów, where we were to spend the next six years.

*Leo and friend, Josef and friend outside
their house in Rozwadów*

2.

Rozwadów
Life in the
Shtetl

ROZWADÓW WAS A SMALL TOWN, maybe around
five thousand people. In the middle of town was a
square – huge, in my memory – where a market was held
once a week. A busy road went right through the square.
Very occasionally we saw an automobile go through, but
the main bustle was the constant traffic of horses and
wagons. I had a good friend, a man who delivered goods
for my father. He had fled the Communists in his native
Georgia and was quite poor. I loved to spend time with
him and with his family. It was fascinating to watch him
as he made ropes. He also told wonderful stories in his
unique Yiddish dialect.

We lived in a terraced house along one side of the
square. At the back of the house was a yard stretching one
to two hundred meters out to a dirt road. We shared a
well with our neighbor. A wood stove heated the house.

There was no running water, and we had an outdoor toilet. It all sounds quite primitive now, but at the time it was normal; everyone lived like that.

My father ran a wholesale business in sugar and other commodities. He bought in big quantities and supplied shops in a large area around Rozwadów. The goods were stored in the ground floor and cellar rooms of our house. We lived in the upstairs rooms. I often listened to him discussing business with my mother. They didn't think I understood it, but I was very curious and took it all in. The problem was always cash flow. People bought things on credit and then couldn't pay. It was a constant worry for my parents.

Occasionally, my father also had stores of candy. At such times I was frequently in the shop at the front of the house asking for some, or begging for money to buy some from another shop down the road. I was a finicky eater, and my parents would sometimes pay me for eating my meals. Father was fairly strict with money, but after Alte Chaiya, my grandmother, came to live with us, I usually got what I wanted. She had first stayed on in Germany, but as we began to hear more and more about what was happening in Germany, my mother finally convinced her to come and live with us.

Alte Chaiya's death was a real blow to our family, although she was well over eighty. She was frying eggs one morning for Leo's breakfast. Suddenly she called our mother over and told her it was time for her to go. Mother couldn't believe she was serious; she hadn't been sick or anything. But Alte Chaiya simply lay down on her bed and peacefully passed away.

Rozwadów was probably half Jewish and half Catholic, and we lived in a mixed neighborhood. The butcher's shop two or three houses away from us usually had pork hanging in the window. One of our close neighbors was Polish, but we had very little contact with them.

There was a strong feeling of community among the Jewish townspeople, in spite of all the differences between rich and poor; in spite of gossip, intrigue, and all kinds of similar things. Jews did not have full rights in Poland, but we were not restricted in our contacts with Poles. I'm sure my parents dealt often with Poles in their business, but as a child I didn't have any contact. In fact, I only learned Polish when I started school. We avoided the Catholic Church, where we heard that they worshipped idols. And we were always afraid of the Christians, especially at Easter. After their church services, they would often go out on pogroms, vandalizing property and trying to break into our shops. So at Easter time, or any of the Christian holidays, we would lock up our shops.

Very soon after we arrived in Rozwadów, my father said to me, "Well, Josef, you have to go to *chaider*." This was the traditional school for Jewish boys. There we learned Hebrew, starting with the alphabet. The *melamet* (teacher) led us in chanting the letters together in a sing-song voice, and he was not afraid to use the stick to keep order. Later, we learned parts of the Pentateuch by repeating after him. We must have learned something there, because I picked up Hebrew quickly when I later arrived in Israel.

We boys were quite a handful for our teacher. The boys had found out that if they formed a line and one touched the live wire in the circuit box, the last boy in the line felt the shock. So that shock was my rude introduction to *chaider* as a four-year-old. If the teacher left the room, bedlam broke out among the fifteen to twenty boys. Even if he was there, some risked beatings to play cards under the table. I remember one older boy who collected money from the other boys by selling each one a tree in Palestine. I never saw my tree, but I certainly learned a few business tricks from him!

When I was seven, I had to go to Polish school, so my parents and my brother and sister taught me to answer a few simple questions: what my name was, where I was born, the name of my father and mother and that kind of thing. In time, I learned the basics of the Polish language and I was quite good in math, but I have no happy memories of that school. Quite apart from the language difficulties, the Polish children, and even the teacher, looked down on the Jewish pupils and generally made our lives miserable.

We didn't often gather as a family for a meal. Mother or Lena would just run up from the shop and cook something for the children. In the evenings, it was a little more gathered. On Sundays, we had to close the shop, so we often went on excursions. Businessmen would go to the river. On Saturdays Jewish people did no business

Josef and Judith at the circus

and we did not walk long distances, but on Sundays and general holidays we took the chance to do this kind of thing. I remember happy family excursions by the San River, and picnics.

I was quite a nervous child with many health problems and I didn't eat properly. I often went to the dentist – probably because of my incorrigible sweet tooth. When I was about five, I had some kind of growth on my toe. Someone told my mother about a man who could help; I don't think he was a proper doctor. He put some powder on the growth and I let out a blood-curdling scream that still rings in my ears. The growth never came back, but I've had a scar from that treatment ever since.

Once I had to spend several weeks in Kraków, where a specialist treated my infected ear. I have terrible memories of how he scraped the pus out of my ear each day. But when we came home, my parents bought me a tricycle. This was quite a novelty in Rozwadów.

When I was about nine, my mother took Judith and me to the Carpathian Mountains for several weeks' vacation. I still have a photo of us standing with a man in a bear costume hugging us. I think this excursion was an effort to improve my health.

We had not actually planned to stay in Rozwadów; my parents still wanted to go to Palestine. Uncle Chaim Simcha and his two boys were already there – I guess they had slipped through before the British tried to stop the influx of German refugees. Father often told exciting stories about what he had experienced in the eight months he was there. He made it sound very interesting and glamorous, so I dreamed of one day going to Palestine, the Promised Land.

3.

Religious Life

CELEBRATION OF THE SHABBAT formed the center of our religious tradition. Friday afternoon, Father took me to the *mikveh,* or ritual baths. First, each one poured a bucket of water over himself and washed with soap. Then we went into a kind of sauna, a steam-filled room with about twenty long steps going up one side. I managed to climb to the fourth step, but the higher steps were too hot for me. After this, we immersed ourselves in cold water. We emerged from the *mikveh* clean – inwardly and outwardly. Then we dressed in our best clothes and returned home for the lighting of the Shabbat candles. This ceremony moved us deeply, and Mother often had tears in her eyes as she lit the candles.

After the candles were lit, Father, Leo and I went to the synagogue for evening prayers. The ancient melodies sung by the *vorbeter* (cantor) pierced my heart. I could understand only a few of the Hebrew words, but the melodies and the feeling of those chanted prayers expressed clearly the persecution and suffering of our people, the longing for God and for redemption. I relive those Friday evenings still today when I secrete myself away and listen to my scratchy recordings of Yossele Rosenblatt.

If any traveler or stranger was at the synagogue, it was considered a *mitzvah* (good deed) to bring him home for the Shabbat meal. Mother always hoped that Father would bring someone along and he often did. Father led us into the house singing, "Peace be unto you from the watching angels," and "Who can find a virtuous woman? Her price is far above rubies." We washed our hands ceremonially and gathered around the festive table. He blessed the wine and then the *challah*. The meal then went on for hours: maybe *gefilte fish* followed by *lokshen mit yoch* and then a dessert. After the meal, Father read to us from Sholom Aleichem or from other famous Yiddish authors. To close the long evening, we sang many prayers and psalms together.

Sabbath morning we slept in. After a light breakfast – maybe coffee cake – the whole family went to the synagogue. Friday evening was solemn, but on Saturday morning there was a more social atmosphere. I loved to watch the reader open the special cupboard where the scrolls of the Torah were stored, pointing towards Jerusalem. He removed the velvet covering in the prescribed way and laid them out on the pulpit in the middle of the synagogue. My father or other men from the congregation were called up for the special honor of assisting the reader.

Sprinze, Mother, Milech, Grandmother, Rahel

There were many rituals associated with the readings from the Torah and the prophets. These were solemnly performed, but a casual, untroubled atmosphere tempered the service. During the long readings, my father sometimes nodded off; another man might then come up behind him, pull on his ears and then pretend that he had done nothing. *Shul* went on for hours.

During all this, of course, my mother sat in the women's part of the synagogue. I think they took it all more seriously than the men. Even though she didn't understand Hebrew, you could see that she felt it in her heart. The younger children could go freely between the men's and the women's sections; often I found my mother weeping.

After a substantial meal, we usually settled down for an afternoon's nap. Sometimes, my father took me with him to the rabbi's house. In some ways, this was the focus of spiritual life for the men. They discussed Scripture and the Talmud with the rabbi. My brother Leo didn't come with us; he was busy with his activities in the Zionist Youth Movement.

When the first stars appeared in the evening, we went again to the synagogue. But the real closing ceremony was held at home. We had another meal and sang praise to God who made the difference between light and darkness, between the sacred and profane. We followed Shabbat – "the queen" – to the door and bid her farewell for another week. Then business started again; we had to think about tomorrow.

4.

Refugees

I WAS TEN YEARS OLD when the war broke out. It broke like a thunderbolt into a sunny summer day. The cultural, religious, and ethnic life of Rozwadów was shattered forever. People were glued to their radios. We soon realized that the invading Germans were advancing rapidly through Poland, and that the Polish army was defeated. Masses of Polish soldiers started retreating through town – among them many Jews. Mother and a few other women set up an outdoor kitchen to cook for the soldiers.

My father's business was destroyed long before the Germans arrived. First, Polish army officers came and requisitioned most of the sugar and rice. They gave us receipts, but even at the time we had no hope of ever receiving any payment. Afterwards, chaos and riots broke out. Mobs of Polish people wandered the streets breaking into shops and looting. They stole everything that was left in our shop.

We feared that the Germans would send the able-bodied men to forced labor camps, so my father and older brother (then twenty-one) fled toward the Russian border. They returned home after about two weeks, however, because the German armies had already moved ahead and closed the border.

When the Germans moved in on Rozwadów, they took the town in a matter of hours. We spent the night in the cellar listening to the sound of explosions and artillery fire. Afterward, my father and Leo hid in the attic; we were instructed to tell the Germans that they had left for Russia.

As a ten-year-old, I didn't understand the seriousness of what was happening. My friends and I ran around town, looking at the soldiers. I remember standing in the square and watching a German officer gather his troops for a pep talk. He walked up and down in front of the soldiers standing at attention. Since German is so close to Yiddish, I understood some of it: "...We have conquered here, and we've conquered there. . . . We have planted seeds in all these countries. Poland is just the beginning. Germany is going to take over the world."

We were not allowed to meet in the synagogue or hold any gatherings. But since it was *Yom Kippur,* we met in one of the houses anyway, to hold our prayers. I will never forget that ardent crying-out to God for his intervention and protection. No one knew what was ahead of us, but everyone feared the worst.

About a month after the Germans arrived, all Jews were ordered to gather in the square within an hour. No one said what was to happen, but we packed all we could carry on our backs. German officers (S.S., I now suppose) ordered us to march towards the San River. They shouted and drove us forward – long lines of men, women and children, all carrying as much as they could manage. One drove by on a motorbike harassing everyone to go faster. He struck my father with his bayonet. I don't think my father was badly hurt, but he fell, and the experience made a deep impression on me.

When we finally arrived at the San, there were more soldiers. I can't remember how we crossed the river, but I remember the soldiers searching us and taking any valuables. As so often, my father had foreseen what might happen and had sewn our money into my younger sister's underclothing. Many people were left with nothing, but we thankfully managed to cross over with some money, as well as fur coats and other valuables.

The eastern bank of the San was a kind of no-man's-land. Apparently, Hitler and Stalin were still arguing over who would take it. There we managed to find some temporary lodging in a village. But it was unclear whether that area would be under the control of the Germans or the Russians, so no one wanted to stay there for long. My father and some other families managed to buy a horse and wagon so that we could move on towards the Russian-occupied area.

Not long afterward, we heard that the Germans were advancing, so we loaded all our goods and some of the younger children onto the wagon and headed east. As we passed through a forest, bandits appeared from nowhere with pistols, and ordered us to stop. We were all frightened, of course, but one courageous man stood up and said, "You can kill me if you like, but we will fight for this wagon." One of his sons stood by him and picked up a stone. The robbers grabbed a bicycle from the cart, but then they went away and let us pass.

As night fell, it was too dangerous to continue, so we retraced our steps a few kilometers to a Jewish-owned inn. Many refugees were staying there. Late in the night, villagers came and surrounded the inn, shouting abuse at us and taking the wheels off our wagons. We were completely surrounded, and I was convinced that these Poles would kill us all. But suddenly, one of the Polish men jumped up onto a wagon and shouted at his peers, "Aren't you ashamed of yourselves for attacking such help-less people? Tomorrow it will be you. Everyone go home! I am standing here with my son, and if anyone touches these Jews, it will be over our dead bodies." This stopped the mob in its tracks, and the crowd slowly dispersed. I have never heard anything more about this man since that night, but I will always have the greatest admiration and respect for his virtue and courage in speaking out against that angry mob.

After about a week, we managed to reach Russian-occupied territory. The distance was not great, but it was slow going. We traveled by day through the forests and rested at night in the villages. The advancing Germans actually overtook us during that week, but they didn't hinder us.

We all rejoiced to see the Russian soldiers at last and to think that we had escaped the Germans. The place – it was called Lanzit, I think – was overflowing with refugees, so we squeezed into a train to Lvov, hoping to find lodging there. Lvov was also crowded, but a distant relative, a merchant, let us stay in one of his storerooms.

We were grateful to have a roof over our heads, but our winter "home" in Lvov was not a happy one. The storeroom must have been about five meters wide and about fifteen meters long. We shared the room with my Uncle Milech and his wife Rahel, but our two families often quarreled. The room was dim and cold. I don't remember a fireplace, but we may have had a wood stove for heating and cooking. Nor do I remember going to synagogue in Lvov; in fact, I can't remember any religious life there at all. I suspect we were all more concerned with survival during those six months.

Our euphoria on first meeting the Russians faded quickly as we saw what life in Russia was like. My sister and I started to go to school during that time. The teacher held classes in Yiddish, but he was a communist and tried to indoctrinate us into the personality cult that surrounded Stalin. I remember one song we were made to learn, which went something like this: "There will always be streams running over the earth; there will always be stars sparkling in the heavens, but Stalin's name will shine over all of that; his name is deeper than the seas and higher than the mountains. There is nothing like him to be found in all the world." Even as children, we felt that such adulation of a political leader was ridiculous; we argued with the teacher, asking, "So who created the world?" But we also had to be careful; people were sent into exile – if not worse – for opposing Stalin.

To make some kind of living, we started dealing on the black market. By watching the shops and standing in long queues, we could sometimes get hold of cigarettes, sweets, and other rare commodities. Even I was sent off sometimes to sell things on the market, especially sweets. I wandered the streets during those months. If I wasn't selling things from a tray, I was mostly jumping trams and doing other stupid things that seem adventurous to a ten-year-old boy. It's a wonder I wasn't killed.

In June 1940, the Russians issued a decree requiring refugees and other non-residents of the Ukraine to register with the police. We were given a choice. If we wanted to stay, they would grant us Soviet citizenship and help us re-settle in the interior of the Ukraine. If we wanted to retain our Polish nationality, they would help us return to the German-occupied part of Poland. After what we had heard and experienced of the Soviet dictatorship, the thought of living under Stalinism was not very appealing. Of course, we had no news of what was going on in the Polish ghettos; in fact, rumors were circulating that life under the Germans was not as bad as people had imagined.

Many refugee families debated long and hard about what to do. In the end, most of the Jewish refugees, including our family, registered to return to German-occupied Poland. We eagerly looked forward to returning home to Rozwadów.

5.

Exiled to Siberia

NOT LONG AFTER WE REGISTERED to return to Poland, a curfew was called in Lvov. We had to wait in our house. Eventually, some soldiers came by with an officer from the secret police. They ordered us to come with them in ten minutes. It was a hot summer day, and we loaded everything we still had onto a truck waiting outside. Then we sat with forty or so other people on top of the baggage and were taken to the train station.

There were soldiers everywhere. We were sorted, somehow, into waiting freight trains – about forty cars with fifty or sixty people in each car. The boxcar had an elevated platform with a primitive hole for use as a toilet; it may have been screened off by a kind of partition. Ours was not the only train; I saw others, and I have heard that nearly 300,000 people were transported that day.

When everyone was loaded, the boxcars were locked shut and the train moved away. It was hot and stuffy, with only a small opening to peer through. We were all terribly thirsty, and there was nothing to drink. We were locked in those freight trains for two or three days, but it didn't take long to realize that we were not heading towards Poland, but deeper into Russia.

After some days, the guards accompanying us opened the cars from time to time and let us out to find food and water. I don't think Milech and Rahel were with us in the same boxcar, but they must have been in the same train, because we all ended up in the same place. Eventually, after about two weeks in the boxcars, we arrived in a Siberian town called Sosva. There we were ordered off the train and herded on foot along a river. Several kilometers farther, we finally arrived at our destination: an isolated settlement consisting of about one hundred log houses arranged in two double rows. This was to be our new home: Camp Forty-Five.

On our arrival, the commandant of the camp addressed us from a platform. He spoke Russian, and somebody translated. He said, "You're probably thinking that you won't stay here long. But I have been here for twenty-five years, and I can assure you that I have never seen anyone leave this place. So you had better get used to it. If you do, you will survive; otherwise you will perish." That was our reception. We were now in "forced exile," a status only slightly higher than that of the prisoners in Siberia's infamous labor camps.

At that time, we were still disappointed that we had been tricked and sent to Siberia instead of to Poland, as we had been promised. But as we later found out, this probably saved our lives. Jews who chose to remain in the Soviet Union were relocated in the western Ukraine, and most of them were later murdered when the Germans invaded. Meanwhile, those of us who had applied for return passage to Poland were by then far from the Nazis, in the relative safety of Siberia. It was one of those times when God somehow used our own foolishness to protect us.

The log houses of the camp had been built by former exiles. Each one had two rooms, and every family was to get one room. My father immediately set about making the best of the situation. He first tried to occupy one of the best houses in the center of the camp, but we were soon evicted and told that it was reserved for privileged residents. So we ended up in the very last house of a row.

Our one room was about five meters square with an old-fashioned Russian woodstove in one corner. My father built a platform for us to sleep on and bartered with other refugees for bricks to improve the stove for heating and cooking. By the time he added a table and a primitive bench, the arrangement was reasonably comfortable.

Our next concern was to gather food and fuel for the winter. Mother took us two younger ones into the forest to pick cranberries. They were plentiful, and we harvested hundreds of liters. Father made a box in a shed outside to dry and store the berries for winter. We also worked very hard to build up a supply of firewood to keep ourselves warm through the long, harsh Siberian winter. Because of Father's foresight and resourcefulness, we managed better than many families. Others later starved or froze when the harsh Siberian winter set in.

Dense forest surrounded the settlement, and the men's main work was cutting firewood. They cut, split, and stacked the wood. Officials would come around, measuring the stacks and calculating wages. Corruption was rampant. Sometimes an official would say, "Give me a bottle of vodka, and I'll let you just move this same pile to another spot. I'll write down that you did double."

Some men worked near our house sawing wood. One man stood on a platform, and they sawed up and down. My father also split firewood for a time, but then he found something better. Near the end of our row of cabins, there were stables for the officers' horses, wagons, and sleighs. My father was paid to care for the animals and equipment. The officers would come any time, day or night, and tell him to hitch up a horse, or they would return a horse that needed to be fed and watered. This was much better work than splitting wood. So it worked out for the best that we had a house at the end of a row.

In early autumn, word went round that all men and all single women were to report for work at another camp several kilometers away, near the river. Father didn't have to go because of his work with the horses, but Leo and Lena did. We didn't trust the Russians and we thought we would never see them again. But they actually did return after helping with the hay harvest.

There was a store where we were free to buy whatever was available. The wages were actually enough to live on – as long as there was something to buy. But as the war progressed, our food rations were cut again and again, until they were so meager that they hardly amounted to anything. My father, however, was not to be outdone. We were not allowed to go more than a few kilometers from our camp, but there was a remote collective nearby. My father knew how to strike deals, and soon he was doing business with the peasants there. I remember going along with him once to a farmer's wife there. He took along an old apron that we had brought from Rozwadów. I thought it was a worthless rag, but my father presented it quite nicely. He made a sales pitch, and finally the woman asked what he wanted for it. My father coolly answered: "Fifty kilograms of potatoes, three liters of milk and some bread." I was so embarrassed, I left the room; I couldn't believe he would ask so much for an old apron. But a few minutes later, he came out with the precious food. It was quite a workout to lug it all back to camp.

Mother stayed home and took care of us children as well as caring for the house. We had to walk several hundred meters to fetch water from a spring. I had to do that chore many times; so did my younger sister. By then, I was eleven and she was nine. Especially when Mother did the laundry, we had to carry lots of water. We boiled the clothes, and I helped with scrubbing them on the washboard and rinsing them out.

As I think back now, I wish I had helped more. There was so much work to do, and my mother suffered excruciating pain from an untreated hernia. At some point,

I started school and began learning to read and write Russian. Ironically, the peasant children had to walk five kilometers through the frozen forest to attend classes at our camp, because their collective was too poor to have its own school.

Our first months had been very hot. Clouds of blood-thirsty mosquitoes tormented us while we picked berries, and we had to be careful not to sink into the swampy mire. But in winter the landscape was transformed. By October or November, everything was frozen solid. Work and school continued as normal unless temperatures dropped below −50°C. My older brother and sister came back from the woods each day completely encased in a frozen cocoon of rags. They had to sit a long time by the stove before they were even able to peel off their clothing. Lena's feet were damaged by frostbite (she has trouble with them to this day because of this) and the father of the family next door to us caught pneumonia and died.

When spring finally came, we planted potatoes. My mother and I did most of the garden work: turning the soil and hauling manure the two to three hundred meters from the stalls where my father worked. We also had to haul water for the garden. The potatoes grew well, and by the end of summer, we were able to harvest a ten-fold return: one and a half tons of potatoes – enough to last for a year.

One day in the spring of 1941, Father came back from his morning chores and said that he was feeling unwell. He was somewhat confused. He lay down, and soon he was completely unconscious, drooling. Mother was beside herself and didn't know what to do. She called to the men who were sawing wood near our house, and they ran for help. One of the refugees was a doctor, and she helped the official Russian "doctor," who had had some medical training, but was certainly no doctor. In any case, the refugee doctor came and prodded Father's feet with needles, but there was no response. She confirmed that he had had a stroke. It was uncertain if he would recover – a terrible situation for Mother.

Leo and Lena were working quite some distance away at another camp, so a man went over to tell them what had happened. He found my sister and told her that Father was not well. At first she did not grasp the seriousness of what he was saying, so he told her, "Look, your father may be dying." She quickly went to find Leo, and they both slipped away and ran all the way to our house – a distance of ten to twelve kilometers. It was dangerous doing this, of course: by deserting their work, they risked being sent to a forced labor camp.

They arrived at home around midnight. In all that time, Father had shown no signs of regaining consciousness, but just before they arrived, he started to stir. What a relief when they burst in and found that Father was still alive! This experience strengthened a real sense of unity in our family. It also brought us close to the two men who sawed wood near our house. They were both well educated; one was an engineer, I think. They had also run quite a risk by leaving their work to inform my siblings. In the end, luckily, no one was punished. (When my brother and sister returned to their work the next day, they learned that the foreman knew what had happened. But he had turned a blind eye while Leo and Lena's workmates covered for them.)

Father slept all day, still drooling. Finally, he woke up, looked around, and recognized us. He had been unconscious for a little less than twenty four hours. He may have been temporarily paralyzed on one side of his face – I don't remember – but very soon he was able to stand on his own again. He was definitely weaker, but not seriously disabled. There was no medication for high blood pressure, so Mother watched him like a hawk to make sure that he didn't get too excited.

By the end of our second summer in Siberia, we heard that the Germans had invaded Russia. At first we worried what this news might mean for us, but it actually brought unexpected relief. Stalin was forced to turn to the Allies for help, and the Polish government in exile used this opportunity to demand the release of Polish refugees held in Siberia. Suddenly we heard that we were free to go as we wished! Of course, we were still stuck in the hinterlands of Siberia, and our homes in Poland were still under German occupation.

Father managed to rent a room in the little town of Sosva about twelve kilometers from camp. This town had a railway station, a post office, and a sawmill where Leo and Lena got jobs. We still had our year's supply of potatoes, so we made many trips back and forth carrying everything to Sosva.

We wanted to get out of Siberia and away from the advancing German army. Looking at a map, we picked Uzbekistan, to the south, as the place to go. We thought that if the Germans took all of Russia, we could flee through Afghanistan and eventually make our way to Palestine. We decided to eat the potatoes and save the rations of bread, since it would be easier to travel with bread.

We dried our bread for the journey in the hot sun and meanwhile lived on potatoes with cranberry sauce. We didn't have sugar, so the cranberries were very bitter. We also didn't have any meat: nothing but potatoes – morning, noon, and evening. For several weeks we had that diet. (Strangely enough, I still enjoy potatoes!)

Finally, we were able to join up with some other families and hire a boxcar. By November 1941, we were ready for the long journey south.

6.

Samarkand: Hunger and Disease

MANY DIFFERENT TRAINS TOOK our freight car along a tortuous route from Siberia to Uzbekistan. As we headed south, trains full of young soldiers were going the opposite direction – toward the front. Of course, military transports always had priority, so we often had to stand several days at some station or another. We used these stops to find food and provisions for the journey.

We never knew when our train might start to move. Once Leo and Lena were returning from an errand when the train suddenly started to pull away. Leo jumped into a wagon near ours, but it took all Lena's efforts to catch hold of the very last wagon. A Russian guard thought she was jumping the train and tried to push her off, but she managed to hang on and argue with him all the way to the next station, where she jumped down and found us.

We heard stories of worse incidents where families were separated for good.

We first tried to find refuge in Tashkent, the capital of Uzbekistan, but the city was completely overcrowded. After a few days, we made our way further south to Samarkand. Here the situation was just as bad. Hundreds of thousands of refugees were fleeing the German onslaught. Many were Jews, though many were not. Father finally managed to rent a room from a Bucharan Jew.* It was small, perhaps two by three meters. At night the six of us just managed to fit on the packed clay floor; we lay there packed like sardines in a tin.

We shared a courtyard and outdoor toilets with the Bucharan Jews who lived in that compound. Their language and customs were strange to us. Even their synagogue was different from what we were used to in Eastern Europe. Later, I heard some speak ill of them. True, some took advantage of us refugees, but on the whole – in our family's case and others – they showed us greater hospitality than might have been expected under such circumstances. They were mostly poor themselves and must have suffered too under the burden of our overcrowding.

Constant, burning hunger gnawed at us through all those months in Samarkand; I had never experienced such desperate hunger. In order to get anything, you had to stand in lines – sometimes overnight. Masses of people waited and pushed forward to receive tiny bread rations.

---

*A common term for Jews of Central Asia, especially in the region of present-day Uzbekistan.

People were crazy with hunger – so desperate that they often attacked those who had collected their rations, snatching the bread and tearing at it on the spot like ravenous wolves. A gang of boys once hit me over the head and stole the bread I was carrying home.

Rumors occasionally made the rounds that a certain shop was expecting a delivery of some commodity or another, and then people would converge and wait for hours outside it, often right through the night. It was illegal to meet outdoors after dark, and the police would brutally disperse the crowds with sticks. But as soon as they disappeared, everyone crowded back. This procedure might repeat itself two or three times during one night. When the shop finally opened, masses of people pressed in. I was small and developed quite some skill at worming my way to the front. Sometimes I was trying to buy a bit of extra food; sometimes, my mission was to procure brandy or some other scarce item that we could resell on the black market.

Somehow we managed to get enough food to survive. Many other refugees died of starvation, or of the typhus epidemics that raged through the crowded quarters. Trucks would pass through the streets each day to collect the dead. Leo was the first in our family to have typhus. He had always been healthy, but now he suddenly came down with a high fever and hallucinations. Mother took care of him; I remember seeing her crying. At great expense, we managed to get a doctor. We tried desperately to keep him out of the overcrowded hospitals where the authorities isolated those with typhus, because the patients there were mostly just left to die.

Then Mother caught the disease, probably from Leo. We were determined to keep her out of the hospital, and prepared to sell everything to pay for a doctor and medicines. We even stood guard at the door in case the health inspectors showed up; when they did, we would lock the door and pretend no one was at home. But Mother's condition only worsened. Worrying for us more than for herself, she sometimes cried out: "What will happen to my children and my husband?" We were all gathered around her bed the night she died. It was the second day of Passover – Leo's birthday.

Mother's death changed my life forever. Her quiet, loving care had held our family together through all those struggles. She had actually spent herself in sacrifice for us. Often she had given up her portion of food so that I could have more. She often needed more help and support than I gave her. How I have since wished to relive those days, to serve her as she served us! But there was only one last service we could do. We went together and buried her in the Jewish cemetery. My father chiseled her name onto the stone marker.

As half-orphans, Judith and I could now go to the Polish orphanage. Father thought we would be better cared for there, so we went. Although we were Polish by nationality and understood the language, we could never really feel at home there. The orphanage was run by Catholics, and their prayers only served to remind us of the pogroms through the Jewish quarters of Rozwadów. It also seemed to us that they prayed to statues – idols, in our eyes – so we kept a wary distance.

Our standard of living was definitely higher in the orphanage than at home. We had clean clothes and more food. But I did not thrive there. After I had gorged myself the first few days, my appetite dropped off. I began to feel sick. I became emotionally numb and began to focus only on survival. I must have turned thirteen in that orphanage, but I don't think I even noticed at the time. My bar mitzvah was lost in all the inner and outer turmoil.

Teheran Children

7.

The Teheran
Children

IN AUGUST 1942, the Polish government in exile made efforts to evacuate Polish orphans from Russia. Many had already died from starvation and epidemics, and the rest were barely surviving. Among some 10,000 evacuated children, there must have been 800 to 1,000 Jewish children. We heard at the orphanage about this chance to get out, and we debated among ourselves what we should do. It was not an easy decision, because it meant that I might never see any of my family again. Later I reproached myself for having left my father.

We were put in trains and brought to Krasnovodsk, a town in Turkmenistan on the Caspian Sea. There we were loaded onto ships. We must have been 10,000 people on that ship; we were packed in as if we were freight. There were no cabins or anything; we just lay on the deck or under the deck. I don't know how long we were on that ship – maybe thirty-six hours. Finally we arrived at the port of Pahlavi, in Persia (present-day Iran). It was summer, so we camped on the sandy beach.

For the first time in many months, we had proper food: mostly corned beef and condensed milk from America. But I was still sick and didn't have any appetite. Soon the Jewish Agency came around our camp, looking for Jewish children. They planned to find as many as possible in Teheran and the surrounding region, and then get them to Palestine. The Allies were always sending supplies to Russia via Teheran and the Caspian Sea, so trucks were constantly going back empty from Pahlavi to Teheran.

We were loaded onto these trucks, about ten to fifteen children in each. The roads were treacherous – very steep, with few places where you could pass, and our way was littered with wrecks. As the truck lurched along these mountain tracks, I felt increasingly sick. I couldn't stop vomiting, and my stomach hurt terribly. I was screaming with pain. At one point I felt so miserable that I tried to throw myself off the truck. Thankfully someone held me back.

It must have taken more than a day to get to Teheran, because we stopped for the night somewhere along the way. Near Teheran, a Polish military camp had one section for Jewish orphans. We were divided up into groups according to age and gender, so I lived with about forty to fifty boys in a big tent, where we slept on mats. In the center of this Jewish camp was a combination store and kitchen where food was provided.

I had constant diarrhea and no appetite. I weighed less than thirty kilograms and was very weak. I was just skin and bones. I looked so pitiful that the Jewish Agency took me around to the wealthy residents of Teheran to arouse their sympathy and raise funds.

Otherwise, I just roamed the camp listlessly or sat with my sister Judith, pouring out my agony. I began to accuse myself of mistreating my mother and abandoning my father. I had nightmares and wanted to die. But Judith loyally tried to comfort and encourage me. She was younger than me – only eleven, and I was thirteen – but I don't know how I would have survived without her. I will always be deeply thankful for how she stood by me.

The Jewish Agency tried to organize us, to provide cultural activities, and to educate us at least somewhat. They provided a team of guidance counselors for every fifty children, as well as the staff who were responsible for running the whole camp. These adults were not all from Palestine: some were also refugees who had somehow managed to get out of Russia and were now assisting the Jewish Agency in trying to help us emigrate.

We had no school while we were there, but the staff taught us songs as we sat around the fire in the evening. Some of the songs I still know today, including *"Arim dem Fajer."*

Among the counselors was a man from Rozwadów, and he recognized me. When he saw the state I was in, he brought me to Zipporah Shertok, a woman whose husband later became Prime Minister of Israel. At that time, she was responsible for the Jewish Orphanage in Teheran. He showed her the skin peeling on the back of my legs and spoke with her in Hebrew. I didn't understand the conversation, but afterward I was told that I had pellagra, a skin disease caused by a lack of protein in the diet. From now on, along with another weak boy, I was allowed into the camp store, and we could help ourselves to anything we liked. We could also order anything we wanted from the soldier's canteen. I always ordered hamburgers and potatoes, and soon I began to gain weight.

Before long, however, I was sick again and was sent to the hospital. They suspected scabies, which was going around the camp, so I was put in isolation. While I was there, news came that we would all be traveling to Palestine. I was terrified that I would be left behind and begged to be released. Just a day or two before the group left, I got out.

We had arrived in Teheran in August 1942 and stayed there for six long months. Now we were leaving for Palestine! The quickest way would have been the overland route through Iraq, but since the government wouldn't allow us to go through, we had to take a roundabout way. First we traveled in a train to a port on the Arabian Sea. Then we were loaded onto a military transport ship bound for Karachi, India (now Pakistan). We traveled in a convoy of fifteen to twenty ships and were constantly on alert. This was toward the end of 1942, so there was intense fighting with the Japanese. Planes sometimes flew right over the ships; it was terrifying.

We slept in hammocks, many children all around. I remember eating marmalade for the first time and learning English songs from the British soldiers. Years later, when living in England, I tried to sing "My bonnie lies over the ocean." My hosts enjoyed it tremendously, because I mixed up all the words. Of course, the sounds meant nothing to me. That was my first exposure to English.

I don't remember too much about Karachi, except that it was very humid and hot. We stayed in a camp on the outskirts of the city and undoubtedly learned more songs and dances from our counselors. By this time I had regained an appetite, but everything was rationed, and so I was always hungry. After three to four weeks, we put to sea again and sailed up past Aden and through the Red Sea, eventually landing at Suez. From there we traveled by train to Palestine.

8.

Palestine

I ARRIVED IN PALESTINE in February 1943. It seemed that the whole country was waiting for us, and we were received with open arms. As our train passed through each station, there were delegations of children and others with flowers, holding them up and greeting us. We were welcomed as the "Children of Teheran." (I don't think we were called that in Teheran, but that is what they called us in Palestine.)

The train from Suez took us to a temporary absorption camp called Atlit, about twenty kilometers south of Haifa. Most of us were used to living as street children. Even during the journey, some of the children had been stealing and getting into other kinds of mischief. We were a rough lot – quite a challenge for our chaperones. But they showed us a lot of love, and slowly they gained our trust. Later on, I think they probably realized that they had been a little too naïve. Thinking of us "poor children," they didn't demand the discipline that they might

Teheran Children arriving in Palestine

have. Whenever some food was put on the table, the children would grab as much as they could, and then hide some of it to eat later or to barter. When they gave out clothing, if the person handing it out turned around, some children would come back and claim they hadn't received any, so as to get more. My most vivid memory of Atlit was a huge heap of oranges. None of us could believe that we could eat as many oranges as we liked. We ate until we were nearly sick.

My dream was coming true; I was actually in *Eretz Yisrael.* It was a tremendous relief to find ourselves in complete safety, but we were also worried about our loved ones – especially our immediate families. We didn't think much about bigger political issues at that time. Like most of the other children, I spent the first year or two in Israel trying to work through all my experiences of the war. I had nightmares and often woke in the night screaming. I was quite nervous and easily lost my temper. It was no different with the other children.

The children ranged in age from one to fifteen, so it was a big job to sort us out. First they tried to identify the various health problems that were rampant among us: lice, scabies, malnutrition, etc. We were sent to different places for recuperation. Judith and I went to Jerusalem and lived in a girl's boarding school called Beit Tseerot Mizrachi. The girls had vacated it and spent six to eight weeks in a nearby kibbutz to make room for us. There we were provided with new clothing and food. They also took us out for tours in a bus. We visited a kibbutz and different sites in Jerusalem and all over Israel.

After about two months of recuperation, they started to decide where we should all go. The mother of Youth Aliyah, a famous Jewish-American named Henrietta Szold, oversaw this process.* She was already elderly, but she had our welfare on her heart and made a point of having each one of us interviewed. She wanted to know about our parents' backgrounds, and what we thought they might have wished for us.

Judith and I were asked if our parents were religious, and we told them they were. Because of this, we were sent to a cooperative called Moshav Sde Yaacov. This was a modern orthodox Zionist village. The people there were

---

*An organization founded by Recha Freier, the wife of a Berlin rabbi, in 1933, Youth Aliyah rescued thousands of Jewish children from the Nazis and resettled them in Palestine, mostly in kibbutzim and youth villages.

religious, though not like the Hasidic Jews, with beards and side locks. They were mostly shaven. They were passionate Zionists, very dedicated. I went to school there and learned to speak Hebrew, which was new for me. (I had learned written Hebrew back in Poland, but did not know how to speak it.)

My best friend during this period of my life was Jakob Finkelstein, a boy maybe a year older than me. The first contact we had had was playing chess as we traveled on the ship to Karachi. Somehow we got into a fist fight and I had ended up with a bloody nose. But after that fight we started a friendship that lasted for many years. We spent hours talking together and also stood up for each other – though I think it was mainly Jakob who took it on himself to protect me in the first months. Jakob also had a sister, Zahava, who was my sister Judith's best friend. Jakob was street-wise and much more savvy than I was and knew how to get the most out of any situation. But it was interesting: on the one hand, he could take advantage of others in a very shrewd, almost cynical way; on the other hand, he was a very faithful friend to me.

In the boarding school in Jerusalem, Jakob discovered that there was a telephone, something virtually unknown to us children in that environment. He wanted to try it out and see how it worked. So he looked up addresses and phone numbers of local religious organizations and, just for fun, called them and told them, "We are being brainwashed here. They are forcing us to give up our religious faith. Can you please help us?" This is the sort of prank we used to play.

Jakob and his sister Zahava were also assigned to Moshav Sde Yaacov along with Judith and me. I was still very nervous and had not found my feet, so I encountered quite a few problems. I was first with one family, but I didn't get along with the mother of the house. They soon put me with another family, but there I had a confrontation with a hired man. He was basically running the farm because the son of the family was fighting with the Jewish Brigades. This man was a refugee from Hungary, in his forties. He was tall and strong, a good farmer – and very devout.

During the time before New Year called *Selichot,* observant Jews get up in the morning and spend time in prayer, seeking God's forgiveness for wrongs they may have committed throughout the previous year. This hired man tried to force me to get up very early – three or four in the morning – and go with him to the synagogue. The first day, I refused to get up. The next day he poured cold water on me to wake me up, but still I refused. As we sat around the table at supper that evening he said, "Now Josef, tomorrow if you don't get up I'm going to do it again." I flew into a rage, grabbed a knife, and threw it at him. I lost my temper completely. Then I hurled myself on the floor, and made a terrific scene. I was shouting, "You're not my father! You have no right to control me!" They were really frightened. Eventually I quieted down, but from that point on he didn't talk with me anymore. I continued to help on the farm, but he ignored me.

Why did I start to rebel against the Jewish religion? I think part of it was my picture of a strict God who is there to punish us. I also felt guilty for my mother's death and for leaving my father in the Soviet Union. I was also afraid.

As it turned out, many other children at the cooperative settlement were unhappy. After eight months, we organized and sent a delegation to Jerusalem with a statement listing our grievances. In response, the Jewish Agency decided to send the older ones away, and the younger ones stayed. Jakob and I went with the older ones (mostly fourteen- to fifteen-year-olds) to an agricultural school at Mikveh Israel. Meanwhile Judith and Zahava stayed on at Moshav Sde Yaacov for a total of about three years.

9.

At the
School of
Agriculture

MIKVEH ISRAEL IS SAID TO BE the oldest Zionist
settlement in Palestine, though there were some Jews
living among the Arabs before that. Charles Netter, a
Jewish philanthropist from France, founded it in 1870 to
train young people in agriculture. This settlement later
became the most renowned agricultural school in the
whole of the Middle East. Besides teaching the students,
the extensive farm covered all areas of agriculture: a dairy
with sixty to eighty cows, sheep, and an orchard with all
kinds of trees. They even had a botanical garden with
many rare plants.

The school had two sections: a religious one made up
mostly of immigrant students like ourselves, and a secular
one made up mostly of students from kibbutzim and
cooperatives. These secular Jews were the majority of the
Jewish population in Israel at the time. The two groups

At the School of Agriculture, Josef and Jakob

lived separately and had separate classes, although officially it was one school.

The "Children of Teheran" were kept together as a subgroup within the religious group. We were enrolled in a two-year course. During the first year, each student was given general exposure to the various branches of agriculture; in the second year, he would specialize in one area for six months, and then choose a secondary branch for a further three months.

Our teachers were also our guidance counselors and tried to help guide us on a personal level. Most of them were modern orthodox Jews from religious kibbutzim. I made their lives hard – I was restless and often a disturbance in class. I was grappling with many questions, also about faith, at the time. On the one hand, I was rebelling against the oppressive idea of a strict God, but I was also beginning to think more deeply about the Holocaust – to ask why or how God could have allowed such a terrible thing to happen.

Some of the other children had come almost directly from the notorious German concentration camp of Buchenwald and told us what had gone on there. They were our age, maybe even younger, but they were like old men – both in the way they looked, and in the way they talked and acted. All of us were shaken up by this.

In the beginning of 1944, around April, our whole class from Mikveh went to Kibbutz Tirat Zvi, a religious kibbutz in the valley of Beit Sha'an. The kibbutz had a work camp: we lived in tents and stayed there for about two months. One day I was standing in line to get food and started talking with a boy who was a few years older than I, maybe eighteen or twenty. When I told him that I was from Frankfurt and that my name was "Nacht," he said that he knew my family. I asked him his name and when he told me, I immediately said, "I remember you, you had a candy shop! It was around the corner from where we lived." He said, "Sure enough!" This was amazing, because I couldn't have been older than four when we left Frankfurt.

This work camp provided me with my first taste of living on a kibbutz, but it didn't impress me much at that time. I was still trying to cope with the experiences of the war, and with my memories of Russia and Iran. When we told people what we had gone through in Russia, they simply wouldn't believe us – they didn't want to. In fact, there was a misguided but deep sympathy toward the Soviets, because they were fighting against Hitler. Many people had an idealistic picture of what was happening in Russia, the land of socialists.

When we returned to Mikveh, some of the other students started a *hachsharah* (group) for the purpose of founding a new kibbutz. They eventually joined Kibbutz Kfar Ezion, south of Jerusalem. (During Israel's war of independence, Jordanian legions overran this kibbutz, and many of them were captured and lost their lives.) Some of my fellow classmates were part of this group, but I was against it. I couldn't accept their piety; I was just too rebellious.

At about this time, I made a conscious decision to oppose religion altogether. I said that I didn't believe in God, I didn't believe in a supernatural power, and I wasn't going to accept anything that I couldn't grasp with my head. I had many questions, and we had heated discussions in class.

As *Yom Kippur,* Atonement Day, approached, everyone in the religious group at the school prepared for the fasts, but as a consequence of my convictions at the time, I decided to break rank. This was no small thing, especially for a fifteen-year-old: among religious people, *Yom Kippur* is perhaps the most deeply revered of all Jewish holy days. But I decided that I wouldn't fast; I would switch on the lights and eat and drink whatever I wanted. I wouldn't have anything to do with it anymore. I told myself that if I felt something was right or wrong, then I

Jakob and Josef

had to act accordingly – not just talk about it – and then accept the consequences.

I was very much alone during this time, except for my friend Jakob. He was in the next class below me, but we still stuck together and talked often. We decided that when we had finished our course, we would leave Mikveh together and help one another. Jakob was more pragmatic than I was. He became secular, too, but only so he could make a go of it in society. He didn't try to buck the entire system like I did. I was always making life hard for myself by following my ideals.

At one point, I even grew violent against the group that was planning to found a kibbutz. A large number of us all lived in the same dorm, but the boys in this group stuck together and ignored me. One day, enraged about something, I went up to one of their ringleaders and hit him, hard. He was shocked – my attack was completely unexpected. Afterward, they ganged up on me and made plans to take revenge. Luckily, some friends found a way to shelter me in the secular part of Mikveh. I stayed there a couple of nights until things quieted down.

Meanwhile, the teachers decided that I was a bad influence and managed to convince me that I should leave the school, though I was only a few months short of completing the two-year course.

In addition, they prohibited Jakob and me from spending time together. (We still met secretly, in the dark. We walked and talked and decided that we were going to stick together, no matter what. I would go out and find a job and earn money, and then he would come out and we would make it together. We would pool our income. Neither of us were interested in agriculture. He wanted to become an electrician, which he eventually did.)

There was another Polish boy at Mikveh named Benjamin Bodner, who had miraculously escaped from a train traveling to a concentration camp and then made his way to Israel. He was also unhappy at the school, and we had talked together about leaving. He told me about the Palmach ("strike forces"), the most elite division of the Haganah, the Jewish resistance. He thought we should enlist, so we went to offer our services. Perhaps I thought there was some glamor in it – I don't know. But I was not very motivated.

At any rate, Benjamin was accepted and I wasn't. I don't know why I was rejected, but I was very high-strung, and a whole year younger than Benjamin. Tragically, he was later killed, during the last days of the war of independence. His father survived the concentration camps and came to Israel only to find that his son had been killed.

At Mikveh Israel we had been trained in weaponry. We learned how to assemble rifles and revolvers. We practiced target shooting. We learned how to climb and jump over houses, and we simulated attacks. We even went out into the desert together and did different military exercises there. At that time, there was a lot of trouble with the Bedouins. They used sticks as weapons, so we learned how to fight with sticks – how to hit and how to defend ourselves. Through that training, I was already an unofficial member of the Haganah, though when I left the school, I lost contact with them for the time being.

Aunt Elsa, Judah, Uncle Chaim Simcha, Sammy

10.

The Search Begins

AFTER I LEFT MIKVEH, I looked for a job. One of the things that I had specialized in at Mikveh was cows. With some help from the college, I got a job at a dairy farm not far from Tel Aviv. The farmer delivered milk into the city with his horse and wagon. People started work early because of the heat, so he had to deliver milk early in the morning – while people were still at home. In the summer I had to get up at one o'clock and milk the cows. In the winter it was three o'clock. He gave me room and board and some small wage. That was my first job. I was very happy to be on my own.

I worked at that dairy farm for about four months, and at first things went well. Then I got into a conflict with the farmer's wife and had to leave abruptly. I told her I couldn't work for her. Once again I was looking for a job.

Luckily, I had some relatives in Israel. My mother's younger brother, Chaim Simcha, was very close to her, and his great love for her extended to me. He had seen, on the list of Teheran Children, that my sister and I were coming, and when we first arrived at Atlit, he came to find us. As we sat in a bus waiting to be driven to Jerusalem, he was suddenly there, welcoming us through the window. He was that kind of a person, very warm and dedicated. Of course, he asked about my mother, but I was not very sensitive. I told him then and there that my mother was no longer living, which naturally gave him a terrific shock.

The house of Uncle Chaim and his wife, Aunt Elsa, became a kind of second home for me. Whenever I had time off in Mikveh or at the cooperative, I could just show up there, and they always received me like a son. My uncle was an extraordinary man with a broad mind. He was religious, but open-minded too, and a deep thinker. He was also well respected, and people often came to him for advice about personal matters or problems in his village.

But even more than Chaim Simcha, it was his son Sammy who influenced me deeply. Sammy was five years older than I, but he always treated me as his friend and equal. When I left the dairy farm, I turned to him for help. I hadn't only lost my job, but my room as well. Sammy had his own place in Tel Aviv; he let me live with him and then helped me find a place of my own. He shared everything with me and didn't make a big thing of it. That generous spirit impressed me very deeply.

Living with Sammy, I met many of his friends. He must have been part of one of the underground groups which had formed to fight the British. Naturally the British jumped on everyone connected with these groups, and at one point Sammy was arrested. I don't think they came up with any charges against him, but he was still sent to a detention camp, as many suspects were in those days, and after his release he was kept on a list of rebel sympathizers. He was also under house arrest and had to register with the police every day. During that time, many of his friends came to visit him at his apartment.

Over the following years I had many, many discussions with Sammy and his friends that changed my entire outlook on life. Sammy did not live for himself. He inspired me to have a bigger vision, to think of others' needs and of the whole world.

At that time I also began to read and think more on my own, especially about the struggle for justice and for brotherhood, about the meaning of life; and I came to feel that I had to live for *something* beyond myself. I had learned enough Hebrew to read when I was fourteen or fifteen, and I can't remember reading any books before that. Now I went to the library as often as I could. I read all the Tolstoy and Dostoyevsky I could find in Hebrew; I bought *Crime and Punishment* and read it through in one night. I surely didn't take it all in, but something stayed with me. The French author Romain Rolland influenced me greatly, too, with his ideals of friendship and social justice – particularly his novel *Jean Christophe,* with its story of Antoinette and Olivier, two orphans who support one another through hard times. It was this story that inspired me in my efforts to join forces with

Jakob, who by then had also left Mikveh Israel and had found a job.

Eventually I found some lodging and work, and Jakob came to join me. I earned £20 a month and rented a place for £10, so I could put aside the other £10 as savings. We shared all the money we earned. I wasn't so concerned about money, but Jakob was more prudent. Eventually we gave up the common purse and divided up the money equally between us, so that none of us had more than the other.

We worked hard, but we also had a lot of fun together. Once Jakob boasted that he could eat two dozen eggs at one sitting, but I didn't believe he could. So I said that if he could eat two dozen eggs, then I would pay for them. He readily agreed, so we went into a shop and bought eggs. I especially ordered extra-large eggs and some bread to go with it – by this time, I was starting to get a little nervous. Jakob ate the eggs, bread and all. I lost my bet.

During this whole time (I was sixteen, and then seventeen), I was really grappling with the meaning of life. What is the purpose of it all? I didn't have a faith, but I was also not satisfied just living for myself. Jakob was busy trying to make a good living and having a good time. However, I thought there was no point in living just to make money and gain recognition. I could see that these things don't make people happy. So we continued to live together, but we slowly drifted apart.

Instead, I was drawn closer and closer to Sammy and his friends. I particularly remember Isaiah and Channah, an engaged couple with whom we discussed many topics. For example, we weighed up the relative advantages of capitalism, socialism, and communism. Issues like this had a real relevance for us as we considered the political situation in Israel – the different parties and their competing ideologies.

Sammy also influenced me with his high standard in personal morals. He was an example when it came to caring for others, but he also challenged people forthrightly whenever there was any kind of off-color humor, or any hint of impropriety. His attitude really made me think about my own values in the sexual area. Actually, he taught me what it means to have reverence for the dignity of others, especially women. Just being in his room opened my horizon beyond the basics of having a job and being accepted by others. I began to look beyond trivial day-to-day matters and to ask myself what I wanted to live for.

I wanted to live for what was right and good, no matter the cost. But I was also torn in two – divided. On the one hand, I felt very weak and incapable of living up to the ideals I was setting for myself. On the other, I knew, deep down, that I could not give up this striving. It may have had something to do with my roots: the calling to live out the prophetic vision of brotherhood that I believe is deeply ingrained in the Jewish heart.

At the same time, the political situation in Palestine was very much on my mind. I was still trying to come to grips with what had happened in the Holocaust. With the war over, thousands of survivors were trying to get into Palestine, but the British were denying them entry. We constantly heard in the news about ships being apprehended by the British and turned back from the ports where they hoped to dock. Thousands of people were turned away; some to Cyprus and others back to mainland Europe. I hated the Germans, but now that the Holocaust was over and I saw how the survivors were being treated, my hatred turned more and more toward the British. (I didn't see the Arabs as enemies – only the British.)

My feelings were shared by many at the time: people regularly shouted abuse at British soldiers, and different underground groups were always attacking them. In return, the British would drive through Israeli towns in tanks; their police stations were like fortresses surrounded by razor wire.

At the same time, I was convinced that people could only be happy by living together in harmony with others. I dreamed of an ideal society where people would live together in peace. I knew that hate had no place in such a world. Nevertheless, I could not forget the Holocaust. I wanted to dedicate my life to fighting for the survival of our people. I was prepared to fight the British by any means necessary.

With Sammy's help, I had found work doing different odd jobs in and around Tel Aviv. I swept streets, dug holes, fixed roads, and did various kinds of building repairs. It was hard physical work. Then I met up with a group that did similar work for the town with a mule and wagon, and got a job with them. I was earning around £1.70 per day and worked six days a week, so that was quite a step up for me. When I got paid on Friday, I would usually go and buy books. I also read a lot from the newspapers as I sat in a café with my workmates while waiting for the next job. I was interested in all that was going on underground, but it was actually more than that. In general, the news of the day enraged me more and more until I felt that I simply had to act.

11.

Fighting for the Land

THERE WERE THREE ZIONIST underground organizations in Palestine at the time I lived there. The first was the Haganah ("the defense"), which later became the Israeli army. The Irgun ("national military organization") was more radical and nationalistic; its aim was to establish a Jewish state on both sides of the Jordan. Many of its members were arrested by the British, and some were executed for terrorist acts. Then there was a smaller group called the Lechi ("freedom fighters of Israel"). The British called it the Stern Group after its founder, Avraham Stern. This group saw the British as the principal enemies of the people and attacked British targets wherever possible, whether military or civilian.

Since I had no immediate family in Israel, I wanted to dedicate my life to fighting for the survival of my people as a whole. I was attracted to the Stern Group and wanted to join it, but I couldn't find a contact. I did, however, manage to get into contact with the Irgun. I was led, very secretively, to a construction site somewhere, and then a strong light was trained on me, and I was interviewed. I could not see my questioners, though they could see me. They asked me, "Do you know what the goal of the Irgun is?" I was quiet. I wasn't so sure what I thought of their aspirations regarding nationhood. My main thought was that we had to fight British imperialism. So I was quiet; I didn't really know what to answer. Besides, I hadn't really wanted to join them; I wanted to join the Stern Group. Then my questioners said, "Shall we tell you what the goal of the Irgun is? It is the establishment of a Jewish state on both sides of the Jordan. Do you agree with that aim?' I said I did, but it was already obvious: I had failed their test. I must have been around seventeen at the time.

In November 1947 a vote was held at the United Nations over the partition of Palestine into an Arab state and a Jewish state. There was great expectation in the country about the outcome of this vote. I remember many people standing in the streets of Tel Aviv listening to the radio as each country cast its ballot. It went on and on, and eventually I went to bed. I lived about three kilometers from the center of Tel Aviv.

In the middle of the night I heard a loud commotion. I realized that the U.N. vote had gone in our favor, so I then got up and managed to catch a taxi into Tel Aviv. The city was euphoric. There were thousands of people roaming the sidewalks. Shops opened and gave out free drinks; people rejoiced. They were literally dancing in the streets.

I stayed in Tel Aviv for the rest of the night. It must have been at six or seven the next day when the reality of the situation hit home – the fact that not everyone was celebrating the birth of modern Israel. An early morning bus from Jerusalem to Tel Aviv had been attacked and many people killed. The reason was simple: while most Jews in Palestine supported the partition of the land, most Arabs did not. They felt cheated and, of course, they made up the majority of people in Israel at that time. They felt that the whole land belonged to them, and that we were there as foreigners, taking away their land. From this time on, conflict started in earnest. (Of course the British had to accept the decision of the United Nations, and they agreed to leave the country by May 15, 1948).

During this interim period, from November 1947 to May 1948, the different underground organizations began to really mobilize. By then, the main fighting was between the Jews and the Arabs. Occasionally the British intervened on one side or the other, but mostly they just let events take their own course. After all, they were preparing to leave.

Throughout 1948, Jewish and Arab groups were fighting all over the country to gain control of different towns and former British police stations.

I was keen to join in the military struggle. Never again would we sit back and accept it when our people were slaughtered, as millions had been in the Holocaust. We would fight for the last inch of Israel, if need be, and establish a safe homeland for ourselves and our children. In

February, I managed to enlist in the Haganah, and subsequently fought in various conflicts until the ceasefire.

I didn't know at this time that my father had safely returned to Germany. Because of this I felt it was better that I should die for the "cause" (rather than someone with parents or children), and I volunteered for anything which looked dangerous. With this in mind, I applied for training in the use of mines and other such weapons. I was no great expert, but I soon found myself in an explosives unit of the Israeli Army. We belonged to the Alexandroni Brigade in the 33rd Battalion.

Around May 1948 I finally managed to get in contact with the Stern Group. I was summoned to a nearby camp and then blindfolded and interviewed. I voiced my opinions about the British Empire – that they would never allow a free and independent Jewish state, and should therefore be resisted. This time my answers were deemed acceptable, and I was invited to join up. Then, just a few days later, the new State of Israel was declared, and everyone from the army was reassigned to his old military unit.

As a soldier I was involved in many incidents. The most serious one took place at a town called Kfar Saba. Part of the town was Jewish, and part was Arab; and our unit was to storm the Arab section. My unit went to lay mines and defend the road from the nearby town of Qalqilya and prevent reinforcements from breaking through. The Arab resistance was much stronger than we had expected.

Within minutes, many of our men were dead or injured. I have vivid memories of comrades dying before my eyes. Then our commanding officer ordered us to abandon the hill and retreat to a nearby orchard. Those of us who had not been hit tried to help the injured. Under heavy fire, we succeeded in moving some of them to relative safety. But suddenly we realized we were encircled by Arabs and isolated from our regiment.

Our commanding officer decided to take a small party back to Kfar Saba to ask for reinforcements. I went along to guide them through the mines I had laid. As soon as we were gone, the Arabs attacked; they killed the wounded soldiers we had just left, and mutilated their bodies. I reproached myself for leaving them there alone, even though there was nothing I could have done to save them. We were all shaken by that experience, but many were enraged as well and couldn't wait for a chance to take revenge.

A few days or a week later we were in action again, trying to take Tantura, a village about thirty kilometers south of Haifa, close to the sea. After fierce fighting, we managed to take control of the town. There were rumors that some men from the village had been killed in revenge for the massacre at Kfar Saba. I never saw any killing, but even the rumor had an effect on me. I wanted to fight for the right to live in this land. I was more than ready to fight against the armies of Egypt, Jordan, and other countries. I was prepared to give my life to secure the existence of the State of Israel. But I was also troubled by how easily cruelty, hatred, bloodlust, and revenge can take hold of the human heart.

Of course, there was no time to think too deeply about such things. At the time, I only thought about how I wanted to do more. In my unit was a soldier named Schmuel Getter. He had come from a group of young people preparing to start a kibbutz, and he planned to re-join it after his stint in the army. The members of Schmuel's group were all part of the Palmach. For my part, I thought I would see more action with them. Schmuel agreed. So the two of us deserted our unit and tried to locate his friends.

That much worked, but there was still a problem: I didn't want to tell anyone that my name was Josef Nacht, because then they would find out that I already belonged to a different unit. So I introduced myself as Josef Ben-Eliezer. "Ben-Eliezer" means "son of Eliezer," which was true. I did this on the spur of the moment, and I have carried that name ever since.

While I was with the Palmach, I mostly stuck with Schmuel and his friends. These young men and women pooled everything they had and held it in common: even though they were all in the army, they had this sort of community within the army. The women kept a supply of all the clothing; you could help yourself to whatever you needed, and then give it back to be washed.

At that time our unit was heavily involved in the capture of Lod, a town near Tel Aviv. Here, my faith in the innate goodness of human nature suffered a serious blow. After the town was conquered, there was an outbreak of fighting in the streets, and soon after that the entire Arab population was ordered to leave. I vividly remember the long lines of refugees – men, women and children – fleeing towards an uncertain future.

At one point, my unit was searching those who were being evacuated for weapons and valuables. The atmosphere was tense, and some of my comrades mistreated civilians. Not surprisingly, my mind flashed back to my own experiences as a ten-year-old boy fleeing our home in Poland. But here the roles were reversed. When one of our men struck a Palestinian with his bayonet, I was stung by the memory of my father being struck the same way by a German soldier. It shook me to the depths: what is it that makes people treat each other like this?

Then I saw two of our soldiers – they were so young, they were actually still boys – take a handful of Arabs and order them to dig a grave. They then forced the Arabs to enter it and took aim at them with their rifles. At that point, several of us shouted at them to stop what they were doing, and they let the men go. Still, I was utterly churned up by the experience: were we really capable of doing the very same things that had been done to us in the previous war? I was in a terrible turmoil. I wanted to fight for the new State of Israel, but only because we were fighting for our survival, not to hurt or brutalize others. (I am certain that the young men from our unit involved in these incidents would never have done such things under normal circumstances, but we were in such a tense situation that moral scruples were easily thrown to the wind.)

During that time I tried to help an Arab who had been forced to dig trenches for us. He must have known some Hebrew, because I remember him telling me that he was a barber. I told him to go home, but he had lost his family among the crowds of people streaming out of town. Again I remembered how our family had fled Rozwadów, and I felt somehow obliged to help him. I walked with him through the narrow streets of Lod carrying my Sten semi-automatic rifle. It was crazy to be out alone like that; I could easily have been killed. In any case, we went right through the middle of town and finally found his family with all their possessions loaded on a horse wagon. I escorted them safely to the edge of town, but I have no clue what became of them afterwards – there was a lot of suffering. On the other hand, there were also moments where kindness prevailed, even amid the general brutality.

Shortly after the action at Lod I fell sick. At first I didn't know what was wrong, but eventually the medics diagnosed malaria. By that time, I was so exhausted, I could barely function. After a few weeks of quinine treatment in a hospital I was able to re-join my comrades, but things were changing. A ceasefire had been declared and there was no more active fighting – at least for the time being. The atmosphere in the unit had also shifted.

We had always had a strong sense of comradeship; the officers and enlisted men were all in it together. But now, the Israeli army was starting to consolidate and beginning to put more emphasis on formal military discipline. Training exercises were strict and mechanical. In any case, I was no longer so close to my friends in the Palmach.

I returned to my unit in the Alexandroni Brigade. Of course, I was arrested for desertion, but the officers were lenient, since I had been looking for tougher action – not trying to evade military service. I was also begging to re-join my explosives unit, which was at that point mobilizing for action in the Negev. This was towards the end of 1948 and was, I think, the last period of heavy action in the war.

Two villages in the Negev were still held by Egyptian units led by Gamal Abdul Nasser, who later became President of Egypt. My explosives unit had a new, untried weapon: a flame-thrower. We had several of them, but it was dangerous, mostly because none of us really knew how to use them. One of them was issued to a young man in my unit named David. He was obviously frightened, and I knew he was the only son in his family. I volunteered to take his place, and our commanding officer agreed. Tragically, David was killed in the first onslaught against Iraq-Manshir – while I carried his heavy, useless flame-thrower all night in pouring rain.

Sometimes I have felt guilty: maybe David would have lived if I had not taken his place. On the other hand, I am thankful for the miracle that I am still alive after deliberately putting myself in danger so many times. Because I was mostly in the explosives unit, I never actually saw anyone killed close up, but I was plagued with flashbacks of comrades dying in battle. Pangs of guilt for my mother's death and my father's unknown fate also haunted me. I could not overcome this inner turmoil, and the malaria only made things worse. During this very difficult time my sister Judith and others of my family went out of their way to support me. So did an army psychologist I visited a few times.

I left the army in January 1949. Of course, most of the fighting was over by then, and Israel was negotiating an armistice with its Arab neighbors. Very soon after that I started to think about all we had done. We had come to Israel and just wanted to live like anyone else – why shouldn't we have that right? But because we wanted to live, it meant that we directly or indirectly caused other people to be uprooted and to live in misery. I came more and more to the conclusion that I could never again cause harm to other people, no matter how noble the cause.

12.

A Reunion

AFTER I LEFT THE ARMY I unexpectedly got back in touch with my father. Unbeknownst to Judith and me, he had managed to make his way back to Germany from Samarkand. Along with Leo and Lena, he had traveled through post-war Poland and Austria, and now he had successfully resettled in Frankfurt. In specific, they had managed to reclaim property there, and also received restitution money. In the meantime both my brother and sister were married. Lena already had a daughter.

My father invited me to join him in Germany. In those days, it wasn't so easy to get to Europe, so no one knew when I would arrive. Finally I managed to book a flight to Paris, and from there I flew to Belgium, and then on to Frankfurt. This was the only connection to Frankfurt in those days – you could not go directly from Paris. (Many years later, I marveled at the massive size of Frankfurt Airport; at that time, civilian air traffic was a fraction of what it is today.) By the time I landed, I was just about penniless; I had only been able to take £10 out of Israel, and had spent most of that already. So I asked for directions, shouldered my rucksack, and hiked off toward the city in search of the address I had with me.

When I finally arrived at Sandweg 46, my father happened to be outdoors, in front of the house. He had barely changed, but the pale, emaciated child he knew from Samarkand had disappeared completely, and he could not recognize me. As I approached, he looked me over, wondering who this tanned young stranger was. Then I shouted, "Father!" and he embraced me; and before I knew it, my brother and sister had rushed out to join us in our tearful reunion. We had been separated for seven years.

As a child, I had not been close to my father. In fact, there had been no lack of conflicts as he tried (in vain) to tame my rebellious nature. In an instant, all that was washed away, without any need to talk about it. He was prepared to do anything to help me. I remember how proudly he brought out an expensive gold watch that he had bought and saved for the occasion. Just to see my father, my brother, and my sister alive helped me to begin dealing with my feelings of guilt for having left them in Samarkand.

My father was doing well: in the post-war confusion, he had managed to set up a lucrative trade in cigarettes and other scarce commodities. He wanted me to join him, but I was independent and idealistic and felt that

Josef, Father, Leo

I ought to live from my own labor, and not by profiting from commerce. I wanted to learn a trade. Before long I found a job laying tiles. I stayed at this job for about six months, until I stupidly twisted my ankle and had to stop work.

Just being in Germany was important for me. I hadn't met any Germans since my childhood, and I had a mental picture of them as maniacs or monsters. How else could they have perpetrated the horrors of the Holocaust? But living and working with them began to soften this view. The master tile-layer I worked for, for instance, was a nice man – a perfectly normal human being. I wasn't naïve: it shook me to think that even a person like him could have been a Nazi, perhaps even a member of the SS. Clearly, pathological leaders like Hitler and Himmler had deliberately committed their lives to evil, but what had made so many "ordinary" people accept this evil and even support it? I had to think of those two young soldiers in Lod. What force is it that unleashes cruelty in the human heart? All I knew for sure was that in situations where there is no moral constraint, human beings can become like animals overnight.

At the same time, I knew that I must never forget what happened in the Holocaust. Two of my cousins had died in a concentration camp; my mother and several other relatives had died of starvation and disease in Russia. I bought a book with photographs of different scenes from the Holocaust. I took it out many times, just to remember. These pictures are still etched in my memory.

More than a half-century later, the pain of it some-times overwhelms me still. I have had numerous oppor-tunities in the last years to visit the Holocaust Museum in Washington, D.C., but I have never been able to bring myself to go. I did once visit the Diaspora Museum in Israel, but I could not stay; the exhibits there were more than I could bear. In fact, the images in my mind are already sometimes too much. I shudder not only for those who suffered during the *Shoah,* but also for those who planned and carried out its terrors. I shudder to think that there is a power at work in the world that brings people to give themselves to such evil.

13.

The Search Continues

I STAYED IN FRANKFURT FOR ONE YEAR, from August 1949 until 1950. I spent all of it with my father and my brother and sister (and their spouses). At first I was happy, but after the accident that forced me to stop laying tiles, I was at loose ends. I hadn't really found my feet in Germany, so I decided to return to Israel. I was by no means a convinced Zionist, but I felt more at home in Israel. For one thing, I knew the language. Further, I felt that I – and every Jew – had some purpose, some destiny to fulfill. This was not a religious conviction – I didn't believe in a God – but I did know that I wanted to live for something bigger than myself.

Back in Israel, however, I began to have doubts. I asked myself, "Why are you always trying to be different from everyone else?" I decided to try fitting in – to conform to "normal" society for once. I looked up Jakob Finkelstein; he had always been much more a man of the world than I.

Josef and Judith

Jakob welcomed my renewed friendship, and we decided to start a business together. I had some money from my father, and he had the business know-how. We bought a few ice cream machines and set up shop. Because

I had been in the army, I was able to get the required rationing permits.

Our little venture was a success, but after one summer I had enough of it. This was not the life I was seeking. Besides, Jakob and I were just too different in character to run a business together: he was quite content to fit into society and get the most out of it, whereas I just couldn't be satisfied with the day-to-day grind.

My whole inner struggle during this time is best reflected in the books, plays, and films that preoccupied me then. Some affected me very deeply. When Lennie loses control of himself and kills his friend in Steinbeck's novel *Of Mice and Men,* he seemed to me to cry out for the need of the whole human race. What is it that prevents people from living in harmony together? The same theme echoed for me through Sartre's drama *No Exit,* where three people are forced to live together and manage to make each other's lives miserable. At the end of the play, one character remarks that "hell is other people." But nowhere was my burning questions more poignantly posed than in Dostoyevsky's *Idiot,* where Prince Myshkin makes his heart-rending appeal: "Why is it that people cannot live together? What prevents them from listening to one another?"

More and more, I grappled with ideals and idealists. I was at a crossroads: the socialism of the Zionists no longer attracted me. I felt that the atmosphere had changed from the days of the early kibbutz movement, when the first pioneers had had to overcome all kinds of dangers and obstacles just to eke out a living. During my time in the Palmach, I had seen the next generation collecting the spoils of war for *their* new kibbutz. They talked about socialism and the brotherhood of mankind, but it looked like plundering to me. After that, I felt I couldn't even contemplate joining a kibbutz.

I started to read a lot of Marxist literature, and had many talks with Sammy. He tried to convince me that the Palestinians would always hate us – as long as we were part of the Zionist enterprise. In a way, he just confirmed my sense that our efforts to establish a homeland could only be realized by disrupting the lives of others. At the same time I argued that one ought to be able to live in Israel and contribute to its building up without participating in violence – by working for reconciliation. He countered that it wasn't our individual deeds or misdeeds that upset the Palestinians: it was the very existence of the nation of Israel, a nation that was displacing them.

More and more, I began to feel that the problem was not a national one. It somehow touched on the whole destiny of humanity. I began to consider the history of the Jewish nation throughout the centuries. On the one hand, Israel was a nation like other nations, made up of human beings like other human beings. Again and again, the people had sought to establish themselves by strength and might. But there had always been Jews who were aware of another task as well: to live out an example of righteousness and justice among the nations. And there had always been prophetic voices calling the people back to this special task. I was still a convinced atheist, but something of all this began to work in me.

Of course, Uncle Chaim Simcha was witness to all my grappling. As I began to feel more and more that I should leave Israel and seek a deeper answer to the need of mankind, he tried to dissuade me. He said that the needs of people are the same everywhere; I did not need to go on a long quest. But I was restless and I felt I needed to leave Israel to find clarity. Finally, he said, rather sadly, "Here is another one in our family who is seeking the Messiah." Perhaps he was referring to his own youthful idealism, or maybe to my cousin Leibich. In the 1920s, this cousin had gone to Palestine, though he was expelled when he became a communist. He had come back to Poland, but eventually went to fight in the Spanish Civil War and never returned.

Maybe there was a special strain of seekers and dreamers in our family; or maybe it is in the nature of our people. I do not believe it is just coincidence that so many Jews have committed themselves to different movements for freedom and justice around the world.

In any case, I began to prepare to leave Israel. I decided to go to Paris. After the war, the city seemed to be attracting more nationalities and ideologies than ever. Perhaps everything would become clear to me there. I hoped to get work as a linotype setter in Yiddish, so I spent six months training for that trade. Meanwhile, I worked night and day to learn as much French as I could. Finally, in May 1953, I left Israel for France.

14.

The Paris Group

My main contact in the French capital was my cousin Berta, who had moved there from Israel a year earlier. Through Berta, I met Jakob Halperin, whom she later married. He headed up a committed group of Leninists in the city.

Jakob was a gifted speaker and could win over almost anyone. He knew Russian, Polish, Arabic, Hebrew, German, and other languages fluently. He was well read and had an in-depth knowledge of classical literature. His hero was Lenin; he criticized Trotsky, Stalin and other communist leaders for betraying Lenin's vision. He was a convinced idealist and dedicated his whole life for the communist revolution. In fact, he was prepared to use almost any means to achieve his goal of a just society.

Looking back, I can see now that Berta and some of her friends in Tel Aviv had spotted me long before as a possible recruit for their circle. Before she left, we had talked about the things that concerned me and about my idea of leaving Israel. But I didn't have any idea that she was involved in such things. I assumed she was being nice to me simply because she was my cousin, and because we shared some similar ideas. Whatever the case may be, I eagerly absorbed her and Jakob's theories once I arrived in Paris.

Jakob's group was marked by its paradoxes. On the one hand it felt like a community: we enjoyed real comradeship, ate together, and shared basically everything. On the other hand, individuals remained fairly guarded. We met for discussions secretly, and never told one another our names or revealed anything about our backgrounds. We produced leaflets to further the cause of "true communism," but these were directed more against Stalin than against the capitalists. We were just a handful of people, but had grand plans: we told ourselves that in Russia, the first communists had also been tiny in number, and yet their movement had thrived. "We have to be ahead of the masses," we told ourselves, "and then everyone else will follow."

I only stayed with "the group" about three months, after which I moved on to live with my brother and sister in Frankfurt. I would have stayed in Paris longer but couldn't get permission to remain in France. During this time, my sister Judith managed to come from Israel for her first visit, so we four siblings finally met again after our scattered odyssey through Europe and Asia.

I must have been in Germany for six months or so, but I never found work and longed to return to my comrades in Paris. Early in 1954, my friends helped me to do this: by devious means I first slipped across the border into Belgium, and then snuck into France. Everything worked out well – until I got to Paris. No one met me at the station as promised, and I didn't have anywhere to go for the night. I didn't want to arouse questions or suspicions by hanging around the station, so I wandered into a neighborhood that had plenty of nightlife. By then, it was quite late, so I settled onto a bench to wait for morning.

After a time, a man came along and struck up a conversation. He was also a foreigner and told me stories about how he had been mistreated. My sympathy grew into stupidity. I told him that I was there illegally. He asked me if I had enough money to get by on, and I assured him that I did, and even showed him my wallet. Shortly afterwards, he wished me all the best and wandered off. Later, I went to buy a cup of coffee and found that all my money was gone – stolen.

The next day I managed to locate Jakob and Berta – a relief – and they helped me find a place to live. In France, you have to register your address with the authorities, so that was a problem. I moved around to different places, but finally a member of our group helped me find something a little more permanent. He was a student and lived in a house where the concierge sat by the door and watched everyone going in or out. He told her he was going back to

Corsica for a time and would like for me to use his room. Each day I went in and out, careful never to say anything more than *"Bonjour, madame,"* so that she wouldn't recognize that I wasn't an ordinary French student. Of course, things got more complicated when I had to pay the rent. Then I had to learn my lines very exactly.

Back with "the group," I continued to occupy myself with the writings of Marx and Lenin. I joined in all the discussions, and attended retreats. Meanwhile my longing for a society where people can live together in harmony – with no injustice and no poverty – grew stronger and stronger in me. Some Marxist theories seemed to provide hope for a solution: for example, the idea that society determines people's behavior. (It is obvious enough that someone who grows up in a slum behaves differently from someone who grows up in a wealthy setting.) So it seemed that if we were to change the circumstances of people's lives, then they would also begin to act differently. For example, if the capitalist system encouraged egotism because of the way each one is forced to fend for himself, perhaps a socialist system that took care of all citizens could encourage sharing and community.

But there were also questions I couldn't find satisfactory answers to. I didn't want to see the disappointing development of communism in Russia repeat itself elsewhere, and wondered how people could ensure that future revolutions would not lead to the same tyrannical injustice I had seen in the Soviet Union.

In the French Revolution, the cry had also been, *"Fraternité, liberté, egalité!"* – but those who seized power later went on to commit terrible atrocities. Their ideas were noble, but was violence really the only way to realize them?

I was also unhappy that hatred was represented as a necessity by the group. I could understand that a revolutionary has to identify with the masses and be willing to fight for them; but to me, that was not the same as having to hate one's opponents. I brought up this issue numerous times with Berta, but she always countered, "What about Hitler?" She had just managed to escape Germany as a sixteen-year-old and had a tremendous hatred for Hitler and the Nazis. I could only answer that though I was ready to kill tyrants and fight for the revolution, it remained wrong (as far as I was concerned) to ever hate anyone – even Hitler. Hatred is beneath human dignity, I told my cousin; it degrades a human being and makes him into an animal. She would only respond, "Oh Josef, you sound just like a Christian – you are becoming a *petit bourgeois.*"

After a few months of this, I felt that once again I had to move on. I did not break ties with the group, but because I had not yet found what I was looking for among them, I went back to Frankfurt. There, I found my brother and sister eager to accept me as a business partner. To their dismay, I wasn't interested. I found construction work – hard physical labor, hauling and digging. It was a tough time. There was no one who seemed to understand me. The unresolved tension was more than I could bear. I occasionally went to a psychoanalyst for help; at other times I turned to alcohol. It was a dark time for me.

Jakob Halperin came over during this time, and I accompanied him as he traveled Germany. His goal was networking the various socialist groups who opposed Stalinism but were still working toward social revolution. Strangely, my heart no longer responded to the ideals he promoted. The vision of a communist society – that is, a cooperative society of equals – still appealed to me, but I was plagued by old doubts and couldn't dismiss what had gone sour in Russia. I wanted to understand why it always went wrong – why, despite the best efforts and loftiest goals, something always got in the way of actually establishing true community. For the time being, I decided, I would try to find happiness by earning my living through my own hard work. Still, I remained lonely – and dissatisfied. I was seeking something *beyond* personal happiness, and I just couldn't seem to find it.

In 1956, I decided to make a go of it once more back in Israel. I was not prepared to participate in war or violence, but despite my earlier scruples, I thought I would try living in a kibbutz. I arrived just as the Suez Crisis broke out. Together with the British and French, Israel had taken over the Suez Canal and managed to conquer the whole Sinai Peninsula. There was terrific euphoria across Israel: for many, it signaled the return to the biblical age of King

David, when the Jews controlled an entire empire. For me it had just the opposite effect: it saddened me.

As I went around the country, I grew more and more disheartened. I still planned to join a kibbutz; at one, I even submitted to the interview for prospective members. But I was too restless, too hopeless to actually commit. More out of despair than conviction, I ended up leaving Israel again to return to Germany.

On the way, I stopped in Rome. I was interested in seeing what attracted so many tourists there. I even went to the Vatican, although it was purely out of curiosity: I was not at all interested in Catholicism or Christianity for myself. While visiting a basilica, the huge doors suddenly closed behind the crowd I was part of, and lo and behold, the Pope himself entered on a litter. As he was carried up the aisle, he raised his arms, and there was complete hysteria – everyone was so excited to be near the Pope. As for me, I found it strangely repelling, even depressing. To degrade someone is always wrong; but I felt that to lift up an individual as if he were a god also goes against human dignity.

When I arrived in Germany in early 1957, I went to Munich instead of to Frankfurt. I'm not sure why. I was severely depressed – even suicidal at times. It just could not go on and on that people hate and fight one another, I told myself. If there was no solidarity to be found among people, then there was no hope for the future, and no purpose in living.

Things came to a real head when I went out drinking one night and someone stole all my money. I was now destitute on top of everything else. I even wrote a suicide note to Sammy trying to explain why I couldn't face living anymore. . . .

A short time later a psychiatrist I went to encouraged me to give it another try; she also gave me some money to get by on and somehow managed to rekindle something inside me. I began to regain hope. Finding a job and working again helped too.

In spite of my bouts of depression, I never gave up my search. I went to courses and watched documentaries about the Hitler years. I was determined to understand how the Third Reich could have happened. When a group of Nazis held a rally in the city, I went, wanting to find out what kind of atmosphere was there. There may have been a thousand people seated at tables in a beautiful hall. Waitresses wandered among them handing out huge steins of beer. A band played rousing, patriotic military tunes, and emotions ran high. Then a man rose to speak. "How can you forget what the Allies did in Dresden? Haven't you heard the lies being told about the German people? Don't you see how our great culture and heritage is despised by these lying hypocrites?" I can't remember his exact words, but he successfully roused the people in that hall.

I looked around and thought of the many who might be unemployed, lonely, or hopeless, as I had been in the previous months. Suddenly it was clear to me how easily things can happen. This man was giving them hope, the promise of a solution for their problems, a sense of belonging. Given the right circumstances, almost anyone could be sucked into the vortex of evil.

AUG · 60

Outing from Sinntal Bruderhof, August 1960

15.

Breakthrough

To FILL MY TIME in Munich and to further my education, I took several classes. One was a course in Esperanto.* I was an eager learner, and once I began reading Esperanto newspapers, I was excited to discover numerous groups concerned with the question of how to achieve peace among the nations. In one of them, I stumbled on an ad from a man wanting to correspond with anyone interested in living a life based on giving what you can and receiving what you need. I wrote to him and soon received a response from an Englishman named Derrick Faux. He told me about an international communal movement he had joined known as the *Bruderhof-Gemeinschaft* ("community of brothers") and informed me that it had recently opened a branch in Germany called Sinntal. He invited me to visit, and I decided to accept.

---

*An artificial language popular in Europe after the war, Esperanto was created by Ludwig Zamenhof, a 19th-century Jewish scholar saddened by the hatred that so often separates people of different nationalities. Esperanto has long been promoted as a way to build tolerance and understanding – a universal tongue to help bring about universal peace.

At this time I was still grappling – constantly – with the question of why people could not live in harmony and solidarity, and why things always seemed to fall apart even when people were committed to the idea of living together. Because of this, the chance to observe a community in action fascinated me. On the other hand, I was skeptical. For one thing, the religious basis of the Bruderhof was off-putting. For another, I was not interested in an island of brotherhood in a sea of injustice and hatred – in a place where the goal is to achieve some kind of personal peace or fulfillment. I wanted an answer that was valid for all people. At the same time, I was in turmoil, because I still hadn't found what I was desperately seeking – and had been seeking, year after year. So I thought: "Well, you can at least learn *something* from a group like this. Maybe you can find out from them why the ideals of justice and equality have not been realized in the various revolutions."

Thinking of the religious and Christian side of it all made me apprehensive, but in the end I went. It was August 1958. I resolved to meet them simply as human beings – without prejudice, and without judging them before I had even arrived. "Be open," I told myself.

My good intentions were put to the test from the very first encounter. I arrived on a Sunday afternoon, and the first person I met was a man walking up and down in front of the house balancing a stick on his head. I asked if this was Sinntal, and he confirmed that it was, without once taking his eyes off the stick. He just kept walking up and down, up and down. I wondered what other kind of strange people lived here – or maybe this one just wasn't quite right in the head – though he did call someone to take me in for a cup of tea . . .

Later that afternoon, a small circus was put on for the children, and the man with the stick appeared as some sort of clown. That explained it: he had been practicing his routine! Still, the whole episode struck me as odd. I was concerned about the destiny of humankind, and here no one seemed concerned about anything more serious than amusing their children.

Afterwards, I was approached and asked what I was looking for – why I had come. On my last day in Sinntal, at a communal mealtime (I ended up staying a few weeks), I was asked the same question again and invited to share about what the visit had meant to me. I said what I always did: that I was seeking brotherhood and an answer to the need of mankind. I said that I longed for this so deeply, I was ready to give my life for it.

I'm sure I also made it plain that I couldn't agree with many of their ideas, but no one seemed offended. Instead, they took a genuine interest in what I was seeking – and obviously saw themselves as seekers too.

I went back to Munich, but once there, I found myself eager to return to Sinntal. In my letter requesting to come back, I wrote, "I long to once experience in my life, in my heart, the answer to the deepest need of humankind. Even if I can experience the answer for only one minute, that will be enough for me." The reason I still remember this particular sentence is that it reflects the intensity of my longing at the time, and its fulfillment: in the years since then, I have experienced so much more than I hoped for.

I came back to Sinntal for a longer visit in September 1958, and again, the members of the little community welcomed me warmly into their circle. We lived very simply: there was practically no heating, and food was scarce. For breakfast we had a tiny block of cheese and some bread to divide among ourselves. At one point the man responsible for buying groceries asked me if I could lend him some money. I gave him everything I had.

I came to love the people at Sinntal, but I also had misgivings and was very outspoken. I respected that as Christians, they had their beliefs – I never made light of other people's convictions – but I wondered why one couldn't live for justice without having a faith in God. For myself, I felt it would be hypocritical to join in their religious activities, so I didn't. Whenever they sang religious songs, for instance, I simply remained quiet. This wasn't easy, because they sang a lot – especially as Christmas approached. But I was principled. I refused to take part in their Christmas play for the same reason. (If a song was non-religious, I joined in with gusto.) Looking back, I am surprised they let me stay. We were a small group with many guests, and it must have taxed everyone's patience, the way I constantly questioned the religious basis of the community.

And in fact, shortly after the New Year, someone came to me and said, "Josef, why do you have to argue so much about the different aspects of our community life, ideology, and beliefs? If you are really looking for brotherhood, *live* it with us. Don't just keep talking about it." Others said the same: they wanted me to take an active part in their life instead of watching from the sidelines as an observer and critic. This made sense to me, and I said I would do it – as an experiment. What I experienced after this, however, came as a surprise.

Because of my whole Marxist outlook, I had long been convinced that external circumstances are what determine human behavior. I believed that once it was achieved, the ideal society would ensure ideal brotherhood. Of course, I had already begun to have doubts, because every effort I knew of to create this ideal society had failed utterly. But when I actually tried living in community, I saw that there was something *inside myself* that resisted it. Slowly but surely, it became clear to me that even under seemingly ideal circumstances, there are plenty of other things that stand in the way of true brotherhood and true solidarity, including the ego, self-will, and touchiness. And these were not the fruits of some outward development or influence, but central to my very identity – part and parcel of every human being. This was a shock. Was my search in vain? What should I do now? I was at a crossroads.

At the peak of my inner turmoil, a man named Heinrich Arnold visited Sinntal. He lived in a sister community in

New York called Woodcrest, and had experienced years of communal living. He seemed eager to talk to me, so I told him my story and what I was looking for. He listened, silently, though with great understanding and compassion; there were even tears in his eyes. Later, in a letter he wrote me from America, he said, "Josef, I trust and believe that one day we will be brothers in the same community." I wondered how he could possibly believe this, since inwardly I was still far from accepting the basis of Bruderhof life. I was still very much a rationalist and atheist; and unready to accept anything whose validity or viability could not be proved.

Whitsun 1959 proved to be the turning point. Many young people, mostly students, came to a weekend conference at Sinntal. Heinz von Homeyer, the well-known author of *The Radiant Mountain,* was the keynote speaker. Of course, Whitsun was a religious festival, and I had my ideas about that. Once again, I was more of an observer than a participant. Then, one evening, I was drawn right into the fray: a heated discussion developed between two opposing camps and soon it was raging so furiously that both sides reached an impasse. I don't remember exactly what the issue was, but by the end, people were just shouting at one another.

Suddenly someone stood up and said, "Dear people, I want to say something. There are two spiritual powers in this world. There is a power that brings people together, and a power that tears people apart. Which power do each of you want to listen to in your heart?" He sat down.

Immediately there was a change in the atmosphere in that room. People were able to communicate again, and many shared freely. The walls that had separated them only moments before had vanished.

Something was happening in that room that I could not fathom. Then it hit me. I can't say why or how it happened, but something struck my heart. At that moment, I felt the reality of the power of the Christ who, through the centuries, has wanted to gather a people in unity, in brotherhood. It was this same vision that the Jewish nation was called to represent, to be an example of a completely new way of life in this world. At that moment, this power completely overwhelmed me and changed my life.

This was the complete opposite of the caricature of Christianity I had seen in the pogroms of Poland, the frenzied crowds in Rome, the self-satisfied Christians in so many places who sought only their own salvation and who persecuted my people. It was not a sweet, personal religious experience; it was the answer to the deep, burning need of humankind – the key to the peace and justice that all people long for. Until that moment, my inexorable insistence on logic had prevented me from being open to any spiritual dimension. But from that point on, I had no doubt. I had found what I was seeking. This was the only answer to the suffering of humanity: to open oneself to the God who loves all people and wants to gather them all to live out his will.

I love the game of chess. In a good match, it often takes a long time before you are ready to make a move. You look at all the possibilities, and then decide. Everything is completely logical; every play is carefully weighed in advance. Still, your opponent may sometimes make a move that you hadn't anticipated at all – one that undoes your whole strategy. In a flash, you realize that your whole approach was built on a false premise, and you have to restart from scratch, as if it were a completely new game. That's what I had to do – what I was given a chance to do – once I found the answer to my seeking.

Postscript

"O people of Jacob, come let us walk in the light of the Lord." (Isaiah 2:5) Let us follow the divine light with all our strength, in trembling, but resolutely. Perhaps in so doing we will be an example, a sign for others, an escape from darkness towards the light. Let us reject the empty boasting to ourselves and others of being the chosen people. Let us show our chosenness through the deeds of daily life, putting into practice what our heavenly Father has called us to be; an example and a splendor to all the nations, to all people.

— *Natan Hofshi*

WHEN A MASSIVE HEART ATTACK took Josef Ben-Eliezer on the night of March 22, 2013, his family – and hundreds of friends around the world – were left reeling by the suddenness of his death. For Josef himself, it was a mercifully swift passage into the arms of a God he had once denied, but later embraced so ardently that even as an elderly man, he glowed with youthful enthusiasm.

Josef's journey from rebellious atheist to committed believer was nothing if not dramatic. On the other hand, his transformation was not so much about becoming a

"Christian" or undergoing a "religious" conversion. It was a matter of having found an entirely new center for his life: Jesus, and his simple but radical teachings about the kingdom of God. No longer consumed by his own desperate search, Josef was now driven by enthusiasm for a greater cause. The irony that this happened in the context of a Christian community, of all places, was never lost on him. But he wasn't one to argue with the way life unfolded. To him, it was simple: at the Bruderhof, among men and women who took Christ's teachings seriously and tried to live by them, he found himself confronted by the God of his forefathers as never before.

The skeptic in Josef died hard – he remained set, for a considerable period, on disproving the viability of community. Over time, however, he found his arguments and defenses gradually melting away. In his own words:

> Up till this time I had claimed that it was nonsense to believe in a higher power. After everything I had experienced and heard, I was indignant that my forefathers brought so much suffering on themselves through their faith in a god.
>
> Like other Jews, I had promised myself that I would never again go like a sheep to slaughter, at least not without putting up a good fight.
>
> Besides, I told myself, there is no God – and certainly no incarnate Christ who suffered with us on the cross of the world, rose, and brings life. It seemed insane to me, through all the things I had heard and

experienced that had been done in his name, especially to the Jewish people but also among the so-called Christians to each other, to still believe in the reality of the living God. I have to say that when I heard the word "Christ" I felt a shudder of horror. In my mind this name was connected to the Inquisition, persecution, hypocrisy, and idolatry.

Yet two years later, he committed his life to Christ through believer's baptism. Shortly after this, he wrote:

Looking back, I see that, all along, my heart longed for God. How ashamed I was when I realized how great his love is, that he let his son be crucified for me! That he never forsook me or gave up on me but rather suffered with me and again and again held out to me his loving hand, that I might understand how great his love is. I still cannot grasp how I could be so blind and could not perceive him, when God's love is so great, even for such a miserable creature as myself.

I had to go through many personal struggles. Sometimes the bottom seemed to disappear from under my feet, but when I felt my own helplessness most strongly – when humanly it seemed hopeless – I experienced Christ beside me most strongly. He never forsook me.

There is no life that does not come from Christ! We have to allow ourselves to be led by him again and again, by expecting everything from him and allowing everything that comes from us to die. And Christ will not disappoint us, even if we often have little faith.

I can only say that I experienced baptism in shame – though also in great thankfulness and joy. Shame, because I had repeatedly pushed Jesus Christ away from me. And yet, his love is greater than our human understanding. It was a tremendous joy for me to realize that this Jesus, of whom Holy Scripture speaks, is alive today as he was two thousand years ago. Everything that was said about his greatness is true, but he is even greater. . . .

Josef added that it was through this discovery of the "real" Jesus – "someone who has very little to do with all the violence that is carried out in his name" – that he realized the promise of a life lived for love and unity.

In my heart I heard Jesus' words, "How often did I want to gather you, and you would not!" I felt the power of these words and knew that it could unite people across every barrier – people of all nations, races, and religions. It was an overwhelming experience. It turned my life upside down, because I realized that it meant the healing of hatred, and the forgiveness of sins.

To Josef, finding faith and a framework in which to live it out was not an excuse for complacency. Decades of living within the Bruderhof community did not dull his urge to reach out to others who might be grappling with the great questions of life – for instance, how to be an effective peacemaker, or how to build a just society. He never forgot the deprivation, hunger, and confusion of his own childhood and teen years, and had compassion for every person embroiled in a struggle – no matter the issue. Nor did he ever forget the desperation that had marked his own journey. Perhaps this is what gave him such passion for the answers he had found, and what gave him the yearning that as many others as possible might find them too. To quote him directly:

> Years ago, in a letter, I wrote, "I long to once experience in my life, in my heart, the answer to the deepest need of humankind. Even if I can experience the answer for only one minute, that will be enough for me." Since then, I have experienced that it is possible for men, women, and children, for Jews, Arabs, Germans, Africans, Americans, and Asians to live together in peace and brotherhood. It is possible to overcome the forces of evil that tear people apart. I have experienced this for far more than a minute. But I still want to give my life for this longing and for its fulfillment.

A few thoughts from Josef's daughter Channah, and from an Israeli friend, Yossi Katz, round out the picture:

> Although my father found a community where people of different races and backgrounds strived to live together in harmony, he never forgot he was a Jew. He would constantly remind us that the calling of the Jewish people is to be an example to the rest of the

world in the sense the prophets had spoken of. In his last years he traveled numerous times to Israel, eager to connect with any group or individual working for a more just society, for reconciliation and peace. He had great respect for each of these people and groups, regardless of their professed belief or non-belief, and always welcomed a good discussion. He had great hopes, too, for the success of the new urban kibbutzim.

To quote Yossi Katz, a professor at Bar Ilan University in Israel:

Josef believed deeply in the choice he had made to join the Bruderhof, but he never hid his connection to Judaism and Israel. To me, this was clearly shown by the names he gave to each of his children, though also by many other things. On a visit to his home in New York, I noticed that his modest library contained the *siddur* (prayer book) *Rinat Israel;* on the same visit, he asked me to send him prayer books for the New Year and Yom Kippur. I once said to him: "You may have left Judaism but it didn't leave you." He smiled that special smile of his and said nothing.

The connection between the Bruderhof and the kibbutz movement was of great importance to Josef, and one of the main reasons for his repeated visits to Israel. On one of them, he joined my wife and me at our home for *Shabbat*. The experience of partaking in this meal, accompanied by songs he remembered from his childhood, and prayers he still knew perfectly, warmed our hearts and our entire house. Afterwards we walked to the home of Hanoch Ahiman, one of Josef's former instructors at Mikveh Israel, who was then ninety. The meeting was very emotional, and the participants wept. Josef had a special love for Hanoch; he felt he was the only one at the school who had understood his troubled heart when he was a resident there. Afterward, every time we met, Josef thanked me for arranging that meeting. Hanoch passed away six months later.

Josef also maintained contact with his sister and brother, who still live in Israel, and met with them and their extended family in 2012. He later told me that he sensed it might have been the last opportunity to meet his brother, who was ninety-four at the time.

Beyond all this, I learned much from him – for example, that the love of a person should not be dependent on anything; about respect for the "other," about the quality of true friendship, and about peace making. He said more than once to me, "Yossi, don't react negatively to those who don't agree with you. Accept it: there are differences."

A particular concern never far from Josef's heart was the ongoing conflict in Israel – and the painful memories of his own role in the earliest years of that conflict. He could still see in his mind's eye the faces of the people of Lod whom his unit had driven from their homes – and, reaching further back in time, the faces of his own people as they were driven from their homes in wartime Poland.

In 1997, almost fifty years after the evacuation of Lod, he came into contact with a Palestinian there named Yacoub Munayer, whose family had suffered at the hands of Israeli soldiers in the upheaval of 1948. After a brief correspondence, Josef traveled to Lod and met Yacoub and his son Salim.

After Josef asked Yacoub's forgiveness for what had happened – a request that was met with warmth and understanding – the men spent time recounting their experiences and trading recollections. By the end of the meeting, they had found complete personal reconciliation. Josef was never grandiose about this personal encounter; to him, it was a modest attempt at peacemaking between two people, set against a daily barrage of stories about tensions and hostilities and suicide bombs and revenge attacks. But as he later said, he had every hope that such a meeting might start a chain reaction. "Violence calls for violence, but by starting another process, by reaching out a hand, finding forgiveness and reconciliation, this could spread. Each of us can do this in our interpersonal relationships: ask for forgiveness and try to build a better world."

The fact that Josef undertook such a trip (he was then sixty-eight) and other similar ones illustrates the way his passion for justice drove him onward again and again, forever searching and never resting or allowing that he had "arrived." At his side, or waiting for him at

Ruth Traub and Josef Ben-Eliezer, England, 1962

home, there was always Ruth, née Traub, his beloved wife of fifty years. She was German – a bookkeeper from Hamburg – and together they had seven children (and a growing crowd of grandchildren).

In a broader sense, Josef was a father to many more than his own children, both within the Bruderhof and beyond it. His sage advice and the humility with which he imparted it made him a trusted mentor, counselor, and confessor to friends and acquaintances from New York to Europe and the Middle East. (Just months before his death, he began mentoring two young Americans doing a year of voluntary service in Bethlehem).

On Josef's eighty-third birthday – his last – he reflected on his life as a follower of Christ and a member of the Bruderhof. Among other things, he said:

It's now over fifty years. How many struggles we've gone through – and I'm still here! One day, though, I will be departing. Don't say, then, that Josef was faithful. He wasn't. But God was faithful. *He* held me, and that's what I want to emphasize today. I tell you, it's the last thing I thought of – not in my wildest dreams – that I would land up in a Christian community. But God led me. God led me together with you dear brothers and sisters, and we are in it together: poor people who struggle each day and fail and stand up again and support one another. We can do this because God is there, and he helps us through. That's why I'm praising God – because he has done this wonderful thing. I'm not so important, but God is great. May we continue to testify – not to ourselves, but to his glory.

After Josef's death, a piece of paper was found in his pocket. On it, in Hebrew, were several handwritten lines:

> I herewith forgive all those
> who have angered or taunted me,
> all those who have sinned against my person,
> my wealth, my possessions or my honor,
> through compulsion, knowingly with malice,
> or in ignorance,
> by their words or by their deeds.
> No one should suffer punishment because of me.*

---

* From the Kriyat Shema Al Hamitah, a fifth-century ritual prayer to be said at evening.

In light of all Josef suffered, especially in his youth, the fact that he cherished such a prayer speaks volumes. At the same time, knowing that he had long let go of any injuries or wrongs done to him in the past – that forgiving was a matter of course for him, and not something he focused on personally – one might wonder why he carried it around with him. To those who knew him best, the answer is clear: it expressed his longing that every person might one day find, as he did, the road to peace on earth – peace for *all* people.

Chris Zimmerman

Other Titles from Plough

Homage to a Broken Man: The Life of J. Heinrich Arnold
by Peter Mommsen. Those who knew him later in life
wondered at the way people were drawn to this man. Few
knew his past or could have imagined the crucibles he had
endured. A remarkable story of faith, forgiveness, sacrifice,
and community.

Salt and Light: Living the Sermon on the Mount
by Eberhard Arnold. Talks and writings on the
transformative power of a life lived by Jesus' revolutionary
teachings in the Sermon on the Mount.

Seeking Peace: Notes and Conversations along the Way
by Johann Christoph Arnold. Plumbs a wealth of spiritual
traditions and draws on the wisdom of some exceptional
(and some very ordinary) people who have found peace in
surprising places.

Why Forgive? by Johann Christoph Arnold.
What would our society look like – and our workplaces
and homes – if people laid aside their grudges and began to
seek reconciliation? Read this collection, and see.

Discipleship: Living for Christ in the Daily Grind
by J. Heinrich Arnold. A collection of thoughts on
following Christ in the nitty-gritty of daily life. Includes
sections on love, humility, forgiveness, trust, leadership,
community, suffering, salvation, and the kingdom of God.

The Plough Publishing House
www.plough.com or e-mail: *info@plough.com*

PO BOX 398, Walden, NY 12586 USA
Brightling Rd, Robertsbridge, East Sussex, TN32 5DR UK
4188 Gwydir Highway, Elsmore NSW 2360 AUSTRALIA